REX

To Laurie, my wife, and my children,

Beau, Mikail and Cole.

KIP

To my parents Wade and Zoe Christensen;

and to my wife Kim and our children, Hilary,

Chelsey, Quinten, Preston and Brittny.

Thank you for your continual love and support.

ACKNOWLEDGMENTS

This book would not have been possible
without the continued support of our families
and help from many mentors and friends.
In particular we would like to thank Dale and
Darrel Nish for their friendship and
encouragement along the way.

We would also like to thank
Jacqueline E. Lee for her help in creating
pens with polymer clay, and Tracy Anderson
for his assistance with machining pens
through ornamental milling.

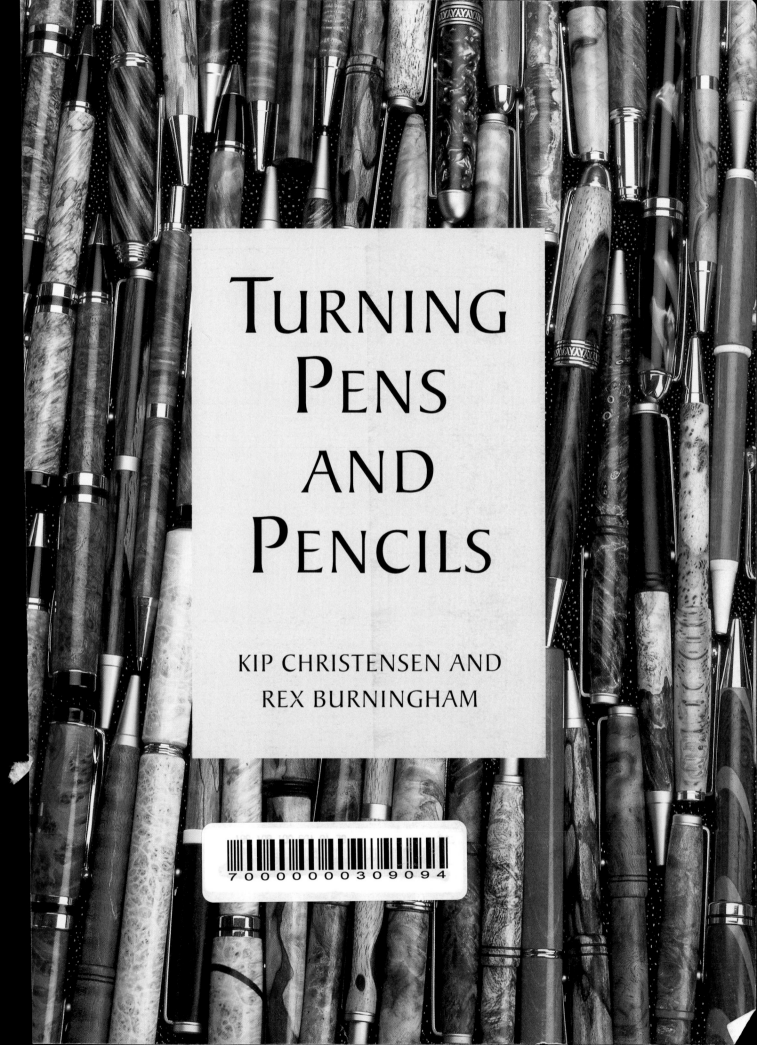

TURNING
PENS
AND
PENCILS

KIP CHRISTENSEN AND
REX BURNINGHAM

First published in 1999 by
Guild of Master Craftsman Publications Ltd,
166 High Street, Lewes, East Sussex, BN7 1XU

ISBN 1 86108 100 6

All photographs by Rex Burningham and
Kip Christensen, except:
Figs 3.1–3.31 and Figs 7.1–7.7 by Dan Haab
Gallery photos on page 149 by Chris Herbert
Front cover photograph by Darrel Nish

Line drawings by Simon Rodway

Designed by Fran Rawlinson

Typeface: Palatino

Color origination by Viscan Graphics (Singapore)

Printed in Great Britain at the University Press,
Cambridge

FOREWORD

Woodturning may be the ultimate woodworking experience for the hobbyist and many turners who make a living from various aspects of the craft. The investment in equipment and tools can be relatively inexpensive and materials readily available from numerous sources. Some may be found, some purchased, some traded for and some obtained from friends who are aware of the woodturner's interest.

A year ago I made pens for my aunts in Canada from caragana (Siberian pea tree), cut from a windbreak planted nearly one hundred years ago to provide relief from the predictable Alberta wind. These trees surround the small, one-room school which my father attended and have been a special source of material for keepsakes and to keep memories alive.

The interest in turning pens and pencils has exceeded the most optimistic predictions since pen and pencil parts were first introduced to the woodturning market.

This book by Kip Christensen and Rex Burningham is the defining book on pen and pencil making. The ten chapters provide a complete treatise on the subject, including history, tools, accessories and materials. The outstanding color photos, with close-up details, are the primary source of instruction, but further clarification comes from the text which expands the knowledge of the reader.

The introductory information is supported with detailed, basic information on the making of straight-barreled pens – the foundation for further adventures in pen making. Further challenges are achieved by following the excellent photos and step-by-step procedures for the very popular European and American style pens. Jigs and fixtures are clearly shown to facilitate drilling and assembly.

Rex Burningham has turned thousands of pens, and has worked to refine as well as design pen mechanisms to make them more user-friendly. He probably knows as much or more about all aspects of pen making as anyone in the business.

Kip Christensen has written extensively, as well as being an innovator in the use of a variety of synthetic and natural materials. His research includes stabilizing spalted wood and working with natural materials such as antler. He is also a proficient pen and pencil maker, with years of wood-turning experience.

Rex and Kip complement each other with enthusiasm, experience and skill. From their combined experience comes the ability to offer numerous tips to help increase efficiency and to prevent or solve common problems in pen and pencil making and suggestions for customizing pen presentation for sales, laser engraving and information cards.

This book is written for anyone with an interest in pen making. It will demonstrate how a novice can be a successful pen-maker, and it will also be an excellent reference for experienced turners who would like to expand their knowledge of pen making.

Dale L. Nish

Contents

INTRODUCTION

Since the mid-1970s the field of wood-turning has experienced an exciting and astonishing renaissance among home craftspeople. Most people participating in the woodturning movement today are doing so for the recreational or therapeutic value they receive from it. Woodturning offers woodworkers a wide range of opportunities to express themselves, from the simple candlestick to the one-of-a-kind segmented bowl or hollow vessel. Unlike other kinds of woodworking, such as furniture-making, which usually requires many hours to complete a project and requires a shop full of hand and power tools, turning allows the craftsperson to produce a finished item in a few minutes' or few hours' time. Furthermore, lathe turning requires the use of few or even no power tools other than the lathe itself.

What other type of woodworking allows a person to make a project, almost start to finish, using only one machine? Yet many a bowl has been made where a rough log section was mounted on a lathe and turned to a finished piece within one or two hours. Woodturning also offers a fluid and creative element rarely found in other types of woodwork. With woodturning, the shape and quality of a piece is determined by the control of hand-held chisels and gouges rather than a mechanical machine set-up. Most woodturning enthusiasts agree that 'the lathe is the greatest tool in the shop' because it takes up little space, requires only a few supporting tools, and offers craftspeople the chance to be as creative as they want. For these reasons the lathe is a perfect fit for many of today's craftspeople.

Of all the new products recently introduced for hobbyist woodturners, the pen has been the most broadly accepted. The popularity of turning pens has snowballed into an avalanche of interest not seen before among turners. In addition to the many attractive features of woodturning in general, pen-making offers several advantages rarely found in other types of turned projects. Turned pens are useful, attractive, inexpensive to make, and are appreciated by almost any recipient. Although they are relatively easy to make, they still offer opportunities to pursue new design elements and work with a wide variety of materials. Pen-making also allows the craftsperson a chance to work in small blocks of time and incorporate into their work common principles of larger-scale production if maximum efficiency is a goal. Since pens can be made on miniature portable lathes, pen-makers can carry their equipment with them when they travel to demonstrate for friends and relatives.

Today's turned pens have evolved from the simple wood pen using a cartridge borrowed from a manufactured pen, such as the one-piece pen with a Bic® insert. There are now over 50 different pen and pencil kits available. The increased interest for pen-making has added new dimensions and opportunities for the hobbyist woodturner, such as the affordability of working with some of the most exotic and beautiful woods the world has to offer without breaking your budget; being able to produce a quality finished product while investing relatively little money and time; the chance to design and express yourself in a creative way; the opportunity to make something of worth that almost everyone needs; the chance to give a handsome gift to a friend or acquaintance without investing significant time or money; and the opportunity to make a little money if desired, or at least recoup your expenses.

In writing this book, it has been our goal to provide a relatively comprehensive yet practical introduction to making pens using a lathe and other related equipment. The book not only includes instruction on turning pens freehand on a wood lathe, but also covers how to make pens using a router and lathe combined, a jeweler's lathe, and an ornamental milling machine. We have also discussed several materials other than wood which turners can use to produce beautiful and unique pens.

It is said that 'a picture says a thousand words'. Throughout this book we have relied on pictures to communicate key information. Our intent has also been to include enough text to describe thoroughly what is being done, and how, and why.

The reader will notice that throughout, we have often shown and discussed several variations of working method to accomplish a similar task. This allows the reader to select the most appropriate procedures based on available equipment and whether they plan to make just a few items or set up for large-scale production.

Throughout the book, we have featured several jigs and fixtures that increase efficiency. In addition, we have included a chapter, 'Tips and Tricks', which provides numerous handy tips learned through extensive experience (see pages 108–132).

Since most people who begin making pens do not stop with one or two, but usually make dozens or even hundreds, we thought it appropriate to address the question, 'What do I do with all these pens?' We have therefore included a section addressing points relative to marketing, displaying and pricing (see pages 133–142).

In selecting which types of pen to feature here, we chose pens that would require a variety of processes and offer different design opportunities. This sampling should provide a good background of transferable information for turners who want to adopt the process for pens of various styles not discussed directly in the book.

The gallery showcase of finished items (see pages 143–156) includes variations of all items covered in the chapters, as well as a sampling of projects that are beyond the scope of the book.

Some photos show equipment with selected guards removed. We have removed guards only when necessary for photographic clarity. We advise that *all* safety equipment be used according to the manufacturer's recommendations.

We suggest that before proceeding to make pens you undertake a careful reading of Chapters 2 and 3, Getting Started, and Basic Pens and Pencils in Detail. These two chapters cover a significant amount of material which is common to most pen-making processes and which is referred to in subsequent chapters of the book.

Making pens is both fun and rewarding. It is our hope that the information in this book may provide you with some fresh ideas – ideas regarding production techniques, the use of a variety of natural and synthetic materials, and variations in design. It has been noted that if wise individuals learn from their mistakes, even wiser individuals learn from the mistakes of others. Much of what is offered in this book is the result of finding a more effective method after having been less successful to one degree or another. We invite you to learn from our mistakes and make a few less of your own. Perhaps this book will help you progress relatively quickly from your present skill level to the next stage, without having to do it all the hard way.

Rex Burningham and Kip Christensen

CHAPTER I

THE HISTORY OF WRITING INSTRUMENTS

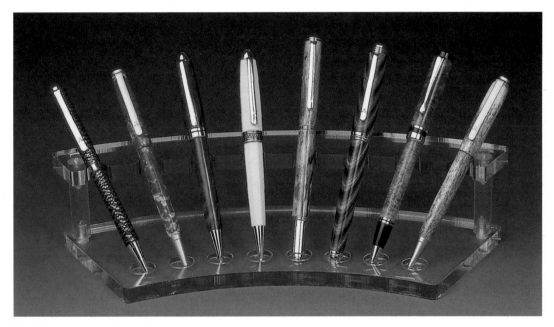

FIG 1.1   A variety of turned pens.

IN BRIEF

Many woodworkers are discovering the joy of making finely crafted writing instruments (see Fig 1.1). The pleasure of making pens is fueled by the simple facts that writing instruments are used and valued by almost everyone and they are a lot of fun to make. A world without writing instruments would be almost unthinkable. Writing is a fundamental form of communication, second only to speech. Writing allows us to record facts, ideas, communications, inventions, drawings, and much more. No doubt writing is one of humanity's greatest and most fundamental developments.

Writing and writing materials have contributed greatly to the progress of mankind and have most probably had an impact on the development of most technological advancements.

Ever since the invention of the most basic ink pen, the pen has had a rich history. Even during our current 'information age', when written and verbal communication is transported instantaneously across continents, and when massive volumes of the printed word are published daily, the pen still remains a basic and irreplaceable instrument of communication.

The first recorded form of written communication are pictures inscribed on cave walls. This type of writing succeeded in capturing the spoken word with the help of pictorial symbols. Stones that were used to scratch into cave walls may well have been the first writing instruments. History suggests that for thousands of years, picture-writing remained the only written language. Gradually the pictures became more stylized and the picture-writing developed into symbol-writing, or pictographs, which could be written quickly with a few strokes.

Papyrus was one of the first paper-like writing materials to be used. The pen used to write on papyrus was a thin reed. The reeds were chewed and then shaped to form a brush on one end. Each reed was then dipped into an ink usually made of a mixture of soot, water and gum. The ink was generally black, but could be colored by using dyes or oxides. The Sumerians and Egyptians wrote on papyrus using a style of picture-writing.

The Phoenicians are known for developing the basic structure of the alphabet. Their alphabet was completely without the kind of symbols that resembled pictographs. Instead, they developed an alphabet of clear, easily written letters. This structured alphabet and a writing material other than stone produced a greater need for a writing instrument, and for a writing fluid to fill it.

INK

'Aleppo oak gall 42 portions and Holland madder 3 portions are diluted with enough warm water to make 120 portions of the liquid. After filtering, one adds one and a half portions indigo solution, five and one-fifth portions iron vitriol and two portions oak gall iron solution.' Such was the description of an ink recipe from the early eighteenth century (*Collecting Writing Instruments*, D. Geyer, 1990, West Chester, PN: Schiffer Publishing Ltd, p. 18).

The search for a convenient and reliable writing ink has been brewing for many centuries. One of the first major advancements was in 1856, when perfume manufacturer August Leonardi was granted a patent for permanent ink. Another refinement was made when an anti-bacterial ingredient was added to the ink in order to stop it from being spoiled by mold.

Another problem was the transportation and storage of ink in small or large quantities. Over the years a wide variety of ideas were developed, ranging from glass bottles of every shape, to leak-proof, metal ink bottles with various types of lid to provide a reliable seal.

The need for appropriate ink storage systems continues to the present day. The inks we use today are the results of many centuries of refinement.

THE QUILL PEN

Sensitive writing materials, such as parchment and thin animal skin, required a soft and supple pen tip. A feather from a raven, peacock, swan or goose was the best. The natural bend of the feather quill fitted well into the writer's hand. Feather quills provided the soft and responsive touch on the parchment that allowed the writer to write with a fluid and elegant motion on the sensitive animal skins.

The rise in trade, and the development of the arts and sciences during the seventeenth and eighteenth centuries, fueled the need for feather quills to new heights. During this period geese were raised only for their valuable pen quills. One goose could supply from 10 to 12 good pen quill feathers.

In the early years of the nineteenth century Germany alone used 50 million quill pens a year. England was reported to have imported 27 million quills from Petrograd in one year, and the Bank of England consumed over 1.5 million feather pen quills in just one year.

In 1809 Joseph Brahman applied for a patent on an invention which was capable of cutting a goose feather into smaller feather pen points. The feather was cut lengthwise and crosswise into about 20 feather points. This finely pointed pen was inserted into a wooden holder. With this invention, the ancestors of the pen point and pen holder had been born.

THE STEEL DIPPING PEN

As England rose to be the leading industrial nation in Europe at the beginning of the nineteenth century, the need to move away from using costly natural materials such as goose feathers increased. Thus the need developed for a pen quill which could be mass-produced by industry.

John Mitchell of Birmingham, England, had the idea of stamping pen quills out of thinly rolled sheets of steel using a steam-driven stamping machine. Over the next several years many improvements took place. Joseph Gillot finally made a steel pen quill in 1830 that could compete on equal terms with the natural feather quill. In 1850, 180 million pens were produced at the Gillot's steel pen factory in Birmingham.

THE FOUNTAIN PEN

The understandable desire to eliminate the necessity of dipping into an inkwell and rather, write with a self-feeding pen is as old as writing with pen and ink itself. The achievement of this dream was attempted as far back as the tenth century. At the beginning of the nineteenth century, the demand for a functioning, self-feeding pen became more and more urgent. For the next 85 years, hundreds of ideas were developed by inventors for how to fill a fountain pen with ink. Unfortunately, the designs were too unreliable and as a result the fountain pen soon acquired a bad reputation.

In 1884, however, Lewis Edson Waterman, a 45-year-old insurance agent, patented the first practical and functional fountain pen. His design worked flawlessly. The ink flowed effortlessly from the pen as if the point had just been dipped into an ink bottle. The new writing nib used a capillary principle to draw ink smoothly into the nib without creating a vacuum in the ink storage reservoir.

The newly invented Waterman's fountain pen caused a sensation. It all came from the street corner of a New York city cigar kiosk, where Waterman personally sold his weekly production of 36 pens. The demand for the new fountain pen soon developed into a production facility in a six-story building on Broadway, and soon even that was not large enough. The fountain pen was born and would dominate the market for the next 60 years.

THE BALLPOINT PEN

In 1938 the first ballpoint pen was patented by the Hungarian inventor Laszlo Biro. This first ballpoint was sold commercially from 1944. Although the new ballpoint pen made many claims about its advantages over the fountain pen, the pens did not live up to the claims. This changed, however, when in 1954 the Parker Pen Company introduced its first ballpoint pen, the famous Jotter. The design improvements in the Jotter made it a worldwide bestseller, and over 17 million were sold per year. With the convenience and low cost of the ballpoint, the era of dominance by the fountain pen was over.

Next to the wooden pencil, the ballpoint pen is probably the most frequently used of all writing instruments. Annual worldwide production of ballpoint pens is estimated at more than one billion. The production methods have been developed almost to perfection, and the resulting high quality has made the ballpoint pen a problem-free writing instrument available to everybody.

TAIWAN'S CONTRIBUTION

Taiwan has developed into the world leader in production of low-cost, mass-produced pens. Contrary to common belief, the success of Taiwan's pen manufacturing is not so much due to low labor costs as to efficient manufacturing technology, and lots of hard work. Most of the raw materials for pens are not found in Taiwan and are therefore imported.

There are very few, if any, manufacturing plants that produce pens from start to finish. Most of the companies selling pens will use subcontractors to produce pen parts, a company may only assemble parts or possibly simply sell them. One subcontractor will produce brass tubes, the next will provide machined parts, another will provide the clips, the next may machine wood tubes, and so on. Some components are imported to Taiwan complete, such as pen refills and pencil transmissions. The success of this type of manufacturing process relies on the ability of subcontractors to be highly specialized, very efficient, and to produce large quantities of quality parts while keeping the cost very low. Taiwan's domination of the manufacturing of low-cost, quality pen components goes unchallenged in today's world.

PENS TODAY

Today, pens are made and sold by the millions in every shape, color, size and style imaginable. Even jewelry, pocket knives, watches and key rings are combined with pens to create the products that we buy. In the current pen market of 'make it cheap', a pen is most often used until it runs dry and then discarded. Fortunately, many people are rediscovering a love of quality writing instruments. Many consumers are looking for pens and pencils that have inherent lasting value; writing instruments made from quality materials, that feel good, look good, and function properly. Not all consumers desire the throw-away pen, but rather a pen that is worthy of using through dozens of refills, keeping a lifetime, and possibly even passing on to an appreciative son or daughter. A finely hand-crafted pen can help fill this need.

THE USE OF WOOD

Wood has always played an important role in writing instruments. The pencil was one of the first to use wood as a method of holding a thin piece of lead. In 1564 lead was discovered by an English shepherd in the hills of Cumberland. This metal material was first used to identify herds of sheep. Before long, the lead ore was cut into thin rods and inserted into wooden holders. Wood casings are still in wide use today.

MODIFIED PENS

In the early 1980s a few craftsmen were beginning to make wooden pens and pencils on a lathe. Most of these were made

Fig 1.2 Hand-turned pencils made from disassembled Pentel pencils. Turned by Nick Cook.

by disassembling mass-produced writing instruments and making a wooden shell to house the components, then reassembling the pen or pencil. An example of this is the type of pencil shown in Fig 1.2. These pencils, turned by Nick Cook, were made from standard Pentel pencils.

One of the most popular hand-crafted pens used a Bic refill and was often referred to as the one-piece pen (see Fig 1.3). The pen consisted of a Bic refill that had been retrofitted into a custom-made wooden shaft. One-piece pens of this style became quite popular among woodturners. The pens could be turned in a number of styles and in any number of woods. The primary drawback with this pen was that the inexpensive plastic refill detracted from the rich wood and quality craftsmanship of the remainder of the pen. For this reason the pen was never broadly accepted beyond the circle of wood enthusiasts.

THE PEN KIT

Sometime around 1989, Craft Supplies Ltd in the United Kingdom introduced one of the first commercially sold twist-pen kits for woodturners (see Fig 1.4). This kit was inexpensive and could be made very easily. The kit consisted of all the metal parts and a refill to make a pen.

In 1990, a pen kit was introduced in the United States by Dale Nish and Craft Supplies USA. It was also received with immediate enthusiasm. In the United States, the craft of turning pens on a lathe was given a huge jump start in 1991 due to an article published by Dale Nish in *American Woodworker* magazine, titled 'Turning Pens: A Touch of Class for the Desktop'.

The instant success of the twist-pen kit soon set in motion the development of all sorts of new styles of pens and pencils. The first pen kit, known as the 'twist pen', was the most basic, but remains one of the most popular kits for woodturners today. When

FIG 1.3 *One-piece pens using a Bic refill. Turned by Paul Fennell.*

FIG 1.4 *Craft Supplies Ltd (UK) catalog and basic kit.*

the pen kits were first introduced, they were marketed solely for use on a woodturner's lathe. But acceptance of the pen kit has expanded to include the general

FIG 1.5 A sampling of catalogs from various suppliers that carry kits for lathe-turned pens and pencils.

but it promises to offer continued opportunities to the hobbyist and full-time woodworker alike.

PLATING

The quality and variety of pen kits has improved considerably since they were first introduced to the woodturner. When the basic twist-pen kit was first offered, it was available in one style only with one type of plating. These kits were manufactured as cheaply as possible. The kit consisted of a very thin, low-quality gold plating. This low quality, however, was matched by a relatively low price.

The success of this low-priced kit was almost instant. Before long individual craftsmen were buying pen kits by the hundreds for between two and three dollars each and selling completed pens for fifteen to one hundred dollars each.

Unfortunately, early production pen-turners soon had two problems to contend with. The first was that pen-kit suppliers could not meet the demands of the market. The second problem was that within a few months customers began to complain that the gold plating on their rather expensive pens was quickly wearing off.

Suppliers soon responded to the concerns of the market by increasing production and by offering a variety of pen kits with higher quality and thicker plating. Today there are several plating options available. Prices range significantly and are generally an accurate reflection of quality. Recently, metals such as titanium and nickel have been added to the list of platings to choose from. In addition, platings are now available in a satin finish as well as the traditional gloss.

woodworking market, which has developed methods for making pens using routers, drills, milling machines and other tools.

The popularity of producing turned pens continues to increase. For some people, pen-making has evolved from a hobby into a full-time business where they earn their living by producing and marketing writing instruments only. The popularity of pen-making is reflected in the wide availability of pen kits. Almost all comprehensive woodworking stores and mail-order catalogs now have some selection of pen supplies (see Fig 1.5). Several businesses are marketing pen-turning supplies only.

The making of hand-crafted writing instruments is still somewhat in its infancy,

CHAPTER 2

GETTING STARTED

SAFETY AND HEALTH

Safety and health should always be of major concern when working in the shop (see Fig 2.1). Those who work around equipment are continually exposed to some degree or another to two types of hazards. One is the obvious hazard of working around machinery that was designed to cut materials much harder than flesh and bone. A finger in the saw blade, a loose shirt sleeve caught in a rotating spindle, and catching a board in the mid-section following a kick-back are examples of the immediate and obvious hazards of shop work.

The more subtle hazards do their damage in an unspoken and unheralded manner over extended periods of time. This includes hearing loss due to prolonged exposure to noise, vision loss accelerated by working under poor lighting, and breathing problems initiated by inhaling fine particles of wood and other materials. Many woodworkers are guilty of carelessness in one aspect or another. Most of us are well aware of the potential hazards. Personal attitudes toward these matters will probably influence the number of years we will be able to work comfortably in the shop using the equipment and materials we so much enjoy.

Near the beginning of each annual publication of the *American Association of Woodturners Resource Directory* there is a list of 'Lathe Safety Guidelines'. These guidelines address several safety and health

FIG 2.1 Protective gear makes working with equipment, wood, and finishes safer and more enjoyable.

issues related to working with wood machinery in general, and woodturning specifically. Topics include clothing, belt guards, running a lathe in reverse, working with defective stock, electrical shock, and others. Similar safety guides are provided by most national woodturning associations. Most of the guidelines given are based on using good common sense when working in the shop. We recommend that you become familiar with the published guidelines and follow them in your work habits. While it is not our intention to repeat all the safety guidelines referred to, we would like to reiterate a few of the items we view as particularly noteworthy.

Proper lighting is something which is often overlooked. Lighting has an effect on the quality of your vision in the short term as well as for years to come. Poor lighting can lead to eye strain that may gradually impair vision. Lighting also affects the quality of your work. Good lighting is important throughout the turning process, but particularly during sanding and finishing. Poor lighting tends to hide defects in work that will surely be exposed later in the light of day as the pen is being used and admired.

Proper safety glasses should be worn and tool manufacturing safety guidelines followed at all times. Loose clothing, dangling jewelry and long hair are of particular concern when using equipment with an exposed rotating spindle such as lathes and drill presses. Take particular care to ensure that there is no chance of anything getting caught in a rotating spindle.

Wood dust is also a primary concern when wood is turned on a lathe. The lathe can generate a large amount of fine dust during the turning and sanding process. Breathing dust over a prolonged period of time may lead to serious health problems. We recommend using an air helmet or a high-quality dust mask and dust collection system to limit the amount of dust that may be inhaled (see Fig 2.2).

Lathe speeds should be appropriate for the size and type of material being turned. Generally, the larger the workpiece, the slower the lathe speed should be. There are various formulas for approximating the correct revolutions per minute (rpm) for woodturning. Generally these formulas are based on the diameter of the stock being turned and may be adjusted up or down to a certain extent, based on experience and sound judgment.

Fortunately, due to the small diameter of stock needed for making pens and pencils, turning the items discussed in this book is relatively safe, even when working at a high rpm. We recommend turning at about 3,000 rpm when turning pens from most materials. Turning slower than 2,000 rpm will decrease turning efficiency. However, if

Fig 2.2   An air helmet is an excellent device for reducing the possibility of inhaling harmful fumes or dust.

you are to err in selecting a lathe speed, it is better to err on the slow side than on the fast side. We recommend that eye protection always be worn when turning any material at any speed. Safety should always be the primary concern when working around any power equipment.

Remember, there may be accidents that smart, but there are no smart accidents.

LATHE SELECTION

Lathes come in all sizes, from huge bowl lathes weighing over 800 pounds (300kg) to the flood of mini-lathes that have hit the market since the mid-1990s. It is generally true that small work can be turned on large lathes, but large work cannot be turned on small lathes. As a result, medium- to large-size lathes – 10in (25.4cm) swing or larger – offer more options to turners. Full-size lathes allow turners to work not only with spindles, but also the full range of turning projects such as bowls and other vessels. Most of the full-size lathes, unless they are specifically designed for bowl turning only, will also work well for pens and other small projects. For general turning purposes, our recommendation would be a full-size lathe.

However, for those who want to do only pens and other small-scale work, the new mini-lathes make an excellent choice. Miniature lathes are relatively inexpensive and require a minimal amount of space. In addition, they are portable, a feature which comes in handy for those on their way to demonstrate at a craft show or needing something to do during a weekend visit to the in-laws.

Since the introduction of the Carbatec mini wood lathe in the early 1990s, the lathe market has seen over a dozen new mini-lathes. This influx of new lathes can make it quite confusing for someone trying to decide which to buy. There are several factors to consider when selecting a mini-lathe. Here are a few things to keep in mind:

- If you already own a lathe that you are happy with, you should select a mini-lathe with similar spindle threads and tapers. This will allow you to interchange your accessories between machines.
- If it is not important to match the thread and tapers on an existing lathe, then select a mini-lathe with a spindle thread that is common to readily available full-size lathes. This will not only increase the resale value of your mini-lathe, but should you decide to buy a larger lathe, you will be more likely to find one with interchangeable accessories. The more common spindle diameters and thread sizes are listed in the following chart. We also recommend that you select a lathe with a standard morse taper. The most common morse tapers used in wood-turning are the No. 2 and No. 1. Most full-size lathes require a No. 2, while light-duty lathes often take a No. 1. Most mini-lathes require a No. 1. However, some of the newer models take a No. 2.
- The horsepower requirements of a lathe are based on the size of the items being turned, which is directly related to the capacity of the lathe. This may vary from $1/4$ to $1/2$ horsepower for mini-lathes and 1–2 horsepower for full-size lathes.
- A speed range should start at around 500rpm or lower on the low end and peak at around 3,600rpm at full speed.
- Consider the general ease of use. With production turning, which is common to small items, it is very important that the toolrest and tailstock adjust easily. Cam action toolrests and tailstocks are the best for quick and positive repositioning. The lathe should have an outboard hand-wheel to slow it down and rotate the work by hand for inspection or sanding.
- If you are planning to turn projects similar to those in this book, the first accessories to get for your lathe are a revolving center with a 60° cone point, and a toolrest about 6in (150mm) long.

COMMON LATHE THREADS

Lathe	Spindle	Headstock	Tailstock
Carbatec I/II	3/4in/16 TPI	No. 1 MT	No. 1 MT
Sears	3/4in/16 TPI	No. 1 MT	No. 1 MT
Myford ML8	1in/12 TPI	No. 1 MT	No. 1 MT
Coronet	3/4in/16 TPI	No. 1 MT	No. 1 MT
Klein	3/4in/16 TPI	No. 1 MT	n/a
Record	3/4in/16 TPI	No. 1 MT	No. 1 MT
Ryobi	3/4in/16 TPI	No. 1 MT	No. 1 MT
Delta/Rockwell	1in/8 TPI	No. 2 MT	No. 2 MT
Powermatic 90	1 1/2in/8 TPI	No. 2 MT	No. 2 MT
Powermatic 45	1in/8 TPI	No. 2 MT	No. 2 MT
General 260	1 1/4in/8 TPI	No. 2 MT	No. 2 MT
General 160	1in/8 TPI	No. 2 MT	No. 2 MT
Oliver	1 1/8in/8 TPI	No. 2 MT	No. 2 MT
**Woodfast	1 1/4in/8 TPI	No. 2 MT	No. 2 MT
Walker-Turner	n/a	No. 2 MT	No. 2 MT
Boise-Crane	n/a	No. 2 MT	No. 2 MT
Atlas	1in/10 TPI	No. 2 MT	No. 2 MT
Jet	1in/8 TPI	No. 2 MT	No. 2 MT
Yates American	1 1/8in/8 TPI	No. 2 MT	No. 2 MT
Harrison Jubilee	1in/10 TPI	No. 2 MT	No. 2 MT
**Vicmarc	1in/8 TPI	No. 2 MT	No. 2 MT
**Teknatool 1200	1 1/4in/8 TPI	No. 2 MT	No. 2 MT
Grizzly G1025	1in/8 TPI	No. 2 MT	No. 2 MT
Grizzly G1067	1in/12 TPI	No. 2 MT	No. 2 MT
Oneway	33mm/3.5	No. 2 MT	No. 3 MT
Harrison	1 1/2in/6 TPI	No. 3 MT	No. 2 MT
Conover	1 1/2in/8 TPI	No. 3 MT	No. 2 MT
Shopsmith	5/8in/Plain	None	No. 2 MT

* TO THE BEST OF OUR KNOWLEDGE!!

**SPINDLE THREADS MAY VARY IN DIFFERENT COUNTRIES.

Miniature metal-working lathes and jeweler's lathes have become quite popular for pen-making (see Fig 2.3). Metal lathes are known for their accuracy and control. The depth of cut is controlled by a hand-cranked feed screw which can be controlled to within a few thousandths of an inch. Using metal lathes takes the guesswork out of making straight-barreled pens, allowing them to be produced very accurately. The only limitation is their inability to do curved shapes, which restricts the craftsperson to projects that have straight barrels. Pens that have tapered or curved barrels cannot be produced on most minimetal lathes without making significant modifications to the lathe set-up.

WOOD SELECTION

Wood for pens must be dry. Unless you know it is dry, assume it is wet. If it is wet, the blanks must be dried prior to drilling. This is best accomplished by stacking the blanks to allow for good air circulation (see Fig 2.4). Then exercise a little patience. Occasionally check the weight of the blanks with an ounce or gram scale. The moisture in the blanks is at equilibrium with your environment when they stop losing weight. (Methods for reducing drying time are covered in Tips and Tricks, see page 108.)

Our recommendation is that plain woods should be avoided and that woods should be selected for striking color and figure. Since it requires such a small amount of wood to make a pen, even the more expensive woods such as the rosewoods, desert ironwood and thuya burl are cost effective. The cost of quality material is usually more than compensated for in increased interest and possible sales. Experience and market surveys have shown that some of the best woods are cocobolo, kingwood, bocote, tulipwood, desert ironwood, and most burl woods. Common woods generally lack the interest of the

FIG 2.3 *Miniature metal lathes are excellent for turning pens and are particularly good for young turners. Here Beau Burningham is shown turning a pen on a Sherline lathe.*

FIG 2.4 *Pen blanks stacked log-cabin style to speed the process of drying.*

exotics unless there is some unique grain or color characteristic. Many common species, that are otherwise rather plain, make excellent pen material if the wood contains burl, fiddleback, feather figure, spalting, or an unusual mineral stain (see Fig 2.5). Often wood can be enhanced by cutting the blank on a bias to the grain to expose additional contrast in color and grain (see Fig 2.6).

Some woods may be of particular interest more because of sentimental or historical value than inherent beauty. Many pen-makers find success in marketing pens from woods indigenous to their area. Examples of this include Texas mesquite, desert sage brush, California almond, English walnut, spalted English beech, Finnish Masaur birch, and others. Occasionally, wood from a tree that has some historical significance becomes available. The alert craftsperson can take advantage of such wood.

Due to the everyday use to which a pen is often subjected, dense woods are more appropriate for pens than softer woods. Softer woods tend to absorb oils from the hand and quickly take on a dull or dingy look. This is particularly true of light-colored woods such as maple, sycamore, holly and box elder. This problem can be overcome by having these woods stabilized through impregnation with plastic resins. Recently, stabilized and dyed woods have become available through a variety of vendors. This material generally makes excellent pen stock (see Fig 2.7).

Some woods that look strikingly beautiful when fresh cut soon bring disappointment due to unwanted color changes caused from exposure to light. The surface color of almost all woods is affected to some degree when exposed to light, particularly ultraviolet light, causing them to become either darker or lighter and less brilliant. In some species this change is drastic and unwanted. Examples include Osage orange, padauk and purple heart. The oxidation process is reduced only by keeping the wood away from light. Since this is not practicable, woods that lose their beauty due to exposure should generally be avoided (see Fig 2.8).

Some of the very densest woods are particularly prone to checking, even after the pen has been turned. Pink ivory, African blackwood, ebony and snakewood are some of the worst in this regard. Checking may be due to the wood not being fully dry, or poor glue distribution between the wood and the brass tube. Exposure to direct sunlight and other heat sources can also cause heat checking in completed pens,

FIG 2.5   *A selection of highly figured pen blanks.*

FIG 2.6   *Pen blanks cut on an angle to the grain.*

FIG 2.7 *Stabilized pen blanks in colored, spalted and burled woods. The samples on the right are both stabilized and dyed, while the samples on the left are natural in color.*

especially if made from exotic woods and 'Dymondwood'. This checking occurs more frequently in the pen styles with straight barrels and very thin wood sections. Suggestions for reducing the likelihood of cracks developing in completed pens are covered in Tips and Tricks (see pages 115, 116–117 and 121). Woods with defects that detract from the pen's appearance should also be avoided. There are, however, a variety of natural 'defects' that enhance the beauty of otherwise plain woods, such as unique coloring from spalting. Working with woods containing these defects often requires special treatment. This is discussed in Tips and Tricks (see pages 126–127).

FIG 2.8 *To show the effects of light and air on these samples of padauk and Osage orange, coins were placed on the face of freshly planed boards and the boards were placed in the sun for several hours.*

DRILL BIT SELECTION

Several different types of drill bit may be used when drilling stock for pens and other mandrel projects. Each has variations in design which make it suitable for specific purposes. Drill bits are designed based on the characteristics of the material to be worked and the required depth being drilled. When choosing a drill bit for making pens, the main consideration is the type of material being drilled. Each of the bit designs discussed below are based on the traditional twist drill used in the metal-working industry.

Standard twist drills with the 120° grind are readily available and come in the largest range of sizes. These bits are designed to drill metal and give good results when drilling material that is consistent in density and has no particular grain direction, such as synthetics. Twist drills, however, tend to wander by following the grain when

FIG 2.9   *The twist drill.*

FIG 2.10   *The brad point bit.*

FIG 2.11   *The bullet bit.*

FIG 2.12   *The parabolic flute bit.*

drilling hard woods with grain that is askew to the hole being drilled (see Fig 2.9).

The brad point bit is similar in design to the twist drill except for the tip. The brad point is specifically designed for drilling wood. The long point acts as a pilot to keep the drill from wandering. Since the point is relatively small, it requires sharpening more often than the basic twist drill. The brad point is an excellent choice for most pen materials (see Fig 2.10).

The bullet bit is another variation of the basic twist drill. Again, the difference between them is the grind at the tip, which leads the way during the drilling process. The bullet point is a compromise between the basic twist grind and the brad point grind. The point of the bullet bit is not as fragile as that of the brad point. The bullet point is designed for excellent tracking in hard materials like Dymondwood and stabilized woods. It generally maintains its edge for longer than the brad point though

DRILL BIT SELECTION

Material to be Drilled	Twist Bit	Brad Point	Parabolic	Bullet Bit
Exotic only	poor	good	good	recommended
Hardwoods	good	good	good	recommended
Burls	poor	good	good	recommended
Bias cut wood	poor	good	good	recommended
Celluloid Acetate (soft plastic)	poor	good	poor	recommended
Crushed Velvet (medium hard plastic)	good	good	good	recommended
Corian (hard plastic)	good	good	good	recommended
Stabilized woods	poor	good	good	recommended
Dymondwood	poor	good	good	recommended
Antler	poor	good	poor	recommended
Alternative ivory, shell, horn	poor	good	poor	recommended

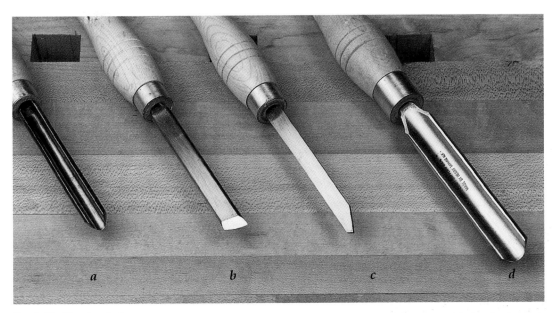

FIG 2.13 Turning tools.

not for as long as the twist drill. At the time of writing, the bullet bit is sold only in fractional and metric sizes and therefore may not be available in the correct diameter (see Fig 2.11).

As the name implies, parabolic flute bits have wide, parabolic-shaped flutes which are designed for fast chip removal. The flutes are also polished to help prevent shavings from clinging to the flute. This bit is very aggressive and works best when the stock being drilled is clamped firmly in place. The parabolic flute bit is excellent for production work (see Fig 2.12).

The chart on page 16 provides a summary that may be helpful in selecting which drill bit to buy for the various drilling materials commonly used for pens. Most suppliers that carry pen mechanisms also offer a good selection of drill bits in the appropriate diameters for each of the various mandrel projects.

Tool Selection

Very few turning chisels and gouges are needed to make quality pens and other small mandrel projects. The tools required vary depending on the project. With careful selection, minimal expense is required to get tooled up for making pens.

When turning pens with straight barrels, some turners can quickly produce quality work using only a $^{1}/_{2}$in (13mm) skew. Others may use a small shallow gouge to remove the bulk of the wood, then make the finishing cuts with a skew.

Some pens, such as the European style pen, require turning a step on the outside diameter to receive a metal band. This step is most often made using a parting tool. Small spindle gouges should be added to the list for turning delicate beads and coves.

All of the projects discussed in this book can be turned using a combination of the following four turning tools, illustrated above in Fig 2.13:

a $^{3}/_{8}$in (10mm) deep fluted gouge
b $^{1}/_{2}$in (13mm) skew chisel
c $^{5}/_{32}$in (4mm) parting tool
d $^{1}/_{2}$in (13mm) shallow gouge

One additional necessary tool is the barrel trimmer. This handy tool simultaneously cleans the inside of the brass tube, while trimming the wood blank flush and square with the barrel. This allows for the metal components of the pen to fit tightly against the wood barrel without exposing any unsightly gaps (see Fig 2.14).

MANDREL SYSTEMS

The mandrel system is used to hold the pen blanks on the lathe while turning. The mandrel allows the turner to work the full length of the stock without interference from a drive center or tail center. Mounted on each end of the pen blank on the mandrel are diameter bushings. These bushings serve as a gage to help the turner size the blank to the proper dimension. The diameter of each bushing is similar to the diameter of the corresponding parts of the pen kits (see Fig 2.15).

If each end of the wood blanks are turned to the same diameter of the bushings, there will be a smooth transition from the wood to the metal parts of the pen. Bushings are selected based on the type of pen and mandrel system you are using.

Bushings tend to become worn and smaller in diameter during use, especially during the sanding process. As a result, if you are planning to turn large numbers of pens, you may choose to buy more than one set of bushings.

There are two primary types of mandrel systems: the one-piece mandrel, and the split mandrel.

SINGLE AND DOUBLE MANDRELS

One-piece single and double mandrels consist of a steel rod that may be mounted on the lathe by any one of several methods. The rod is threaded on the tailstock end to receive a nut that secures the stock and

FIG 2.14 *The barrel trimmer at the bottom of the photo can be chucked in a hand drill. When the barrel trimmer is mounted in a simple turned handle, it can be used by hand without the use of power tools.*

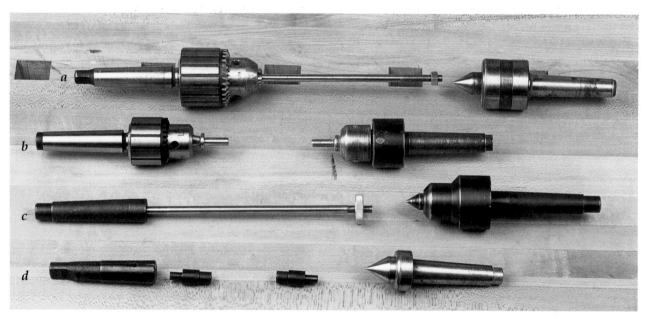

FIG 2.15 *Shown here are several mandrel systems: (a) single mandrel in a drill chuck; (b) split mandrel or mandrel points held in a drill chuck; (c) No. 2 morse taper double mandrel; (d) mandrel points in a drill driver.*

bushings firmly in place. The rod is also dimpled on the same end to receive the tip of a revolving cone center. The pen blanks are slid onto the mandrel with a diameter bushing at each end of the stock and secured in place with the nut.

The single mandrel is approximately half the length of the double mandrel and is designed to mount only one half of a pen at a time. The single mandrel offers the advantage of being more rigid and less likely to flex than the longer double mandrel. This allows the turner to be more aggressive, particularly during the roughing stage. The disadvantage of using the single mandrel is the additional time that is required in order to mount and turn each pen barrel separately.

The double mandrel is long enough so that both pen barrels can be mounted and turned in a single operation. This reduces the time required for set-up. The longer mandrel, however, is more prone to problems. If the headstock and tailstock of the lathe are out of alignment, the double mandrel tends to accentuate the problem. This results in an uneven wall thickness in the wood around the tube. Over-tightening the tailstock or the mandrel nut can also cause the mandrel to flex and not run true.

Mandrels may be mounted in the headstock of the lathe using a variety of methods. The most common method is to have the mandrel threaded directly into a morse taper (see Fig 2.15c). Other methods include a drill chuck (see Fig 2.15a/b), and a drill driver (see Fig 2.15d). In each case a revolving center, that will spin with the mandrel as the spindle rotates, supports the mandrel in the tailstock.

Morse taper mandrel systems are designed to work with most standard wood lathes. The taper fits directly into the spindle at the headstock of the lathe.

A drill chuck without a morse taper can also be used to hold a mandrel. It can accept a single or double mandrel. This method is used when your lathe is not equipped with a morse taper, for example a Shopsmith lathe. In this case, the drill chuck is fastened directly onto the spindle.

SPLIT MANDRELS

Split mandrels, or mandrel points, do not use the rod system but rather consist of two mandrel points that fit inside the ends of a barrel. One mandrel point is mounted in the headstock while the other is mounted in the tailstock. The mandrel point at the headstock end may be secured in a morse taper, a drill chuck, or a drill driver. Diameter bushings are placed around each mandrel point.

The split mandrel is designed to mount one barrel at a time. As with the single, one-piece mandrel, this permits the turner to be quite aggressive.

One distinct advantage that the split mandrel gives over the single mandrel is the speed and ease of mounting and dismounting barrels. The split mandrel system uses the tailstock, rather than a mandrel nut, to tighten the blanks on the mandrels for turning.

Drill drivers are designed to clamp down on the single or double mandrel or on the mandrel points as the drill driver is fitted into the spindle. Drill drivers are available in a No. 1 MT or No. 2 MT and double or single mandrels.

It should be emphasized that, when buying mandrels and pen kits, you should be sure to check with your supplier to make sure that the items will be compatible with your particular lathe.

There are currently several reliable suppliers of kits for pens and other mandrel projects. Throughout the chapters of this book are items made from kits carried by a variety of suppliers. In addition to the major suppliers, many local woodworking stores carry kits for pens and mandrel projects. Your local phone directory may help you to locate suppliers in your area.

ADHESIVES

Choosing the proper adhesive is crucial. Adhesives used for making pens must adhere to the metal tube, be somewhat flexible after curing, and also have some gap-filling properties. Gluing the tube into the blank is one of the most important steps in pen-making. An error in this step can lead to failure in three different ways. The first comes while turning the blank. Improper gluing may cause the wood to tear away from the brass tube due to a starved glue joint between the tube and the wood. Second, the wood barrel may crack during the final assembly of the pen. This is due to the glue and wood being very brittle and not having the needed flexibility to expand slightly without cracking. Finally, the blank may crack due to heat or direct sunlight after the pen is in use.

Below is a brief description of three types of adhesive that meet the needed characteristics mentioned above. These include cyanoacrylate, epoxy and polyurethane glue. In order to select the best adhesive for the material being glued it is important to become familiar with the characteristics of each of the adhesives (see Fig 2.16 and the table on page 21).

Cyanoacrylate (CA) is available in thin and thick consistencies, both of which are very useful and are a must for the woodturner's shop. Gap-filling CA has a syrup consistency and is excellent for gluing the tubes to the stock. It can also be used for repairing small cracks and defects in the wood. This process is shown in Tips and Tricks (see page 126). CA is the most costly of the recommended adhesives. Thin CA has a viscosity similar to that of water. It is often used to strengthen soft woods and can also be used as a finish. Thin CA lacks the ability to fill gaps and therefore is not recommended for gluing in the brass tube. Cyanoacrylate accelerator is often used to quickly harden exposed surface glue.

Epoxy adhesives have excellent gap-filling properties, remain sufficiently flexible after curing, and give excellent results when gluing brass tubes into blanks. Epoxies are two-part adhesives and require mixing just prior to application. As the name implies, five-minute epoxy gives about five minutes of working time. It requires about 30 minutes of curing time before the blank can be turned. Slow-setting epoxy offers a longer working time but requires 6–12 hours before machining can begin. When cured, slow-setting epoxy will remain more

FIG 2.16 *A variety of adhesives that are excellent for gluing the brass tube into the pen blank.*

Material	Cyanoacrylate	Five-Minute Epoxy	Slow-Set Epoxy	Polyurethane
Exotic oily	yes	yes	yes	yes
Hard woods	yes	yes	yes	yes
Burls	yes	yes	yes	yes
Basis cut wood	yes	yes	yes	yes
Celluloid Acetate (soft plastic)	–	yes	yes	–
Crushed Velvet (medium hard)	yes	yes	yes	yes
Corian (hard plastics)	–	yes	yes	yes
Impregnated woods	yes	yes	yes	yes
Dymondwood	yes	yes	yes	yes
Antler	yes	yes	yes	–
Alternative ivory, shell, horn	–	yes	yes	yes
Property				
Flexibility	poor	good	good	excellent
Relative cost	high	low	low	low
Ease of use	fair	good	good	best
Setting time	5 mins	30 mins	6 -12 hours	8 -12 hours

flexible than five-minute epoxy or cyanoacrylate glues.

Polyurethane glue has some excellent features for gluing tubes into the wood. It is waterproof, very flexible, expands to fill gaps, and is relatively inexpensive. The glue has a 20–30 minute working time and requires 8–12 hours to cure.

The chart above indicates recommended adhesives in relation to gluing various materials and other factors of interest.

ABRASIVES

Today a wide variety of abrasives are available. Many of these are designed for very specific uses which are not of particular interest to the woodturner. For our purposes here, we will limit our discussion to a summary of basic concepts that may influence woodturners in selecting which abrasive to use. Abrasives are selected based on five variables: type of abrasive material, type of backing, the weight of the backing material, type of adhesive that bonds the abrasive grit to the backing, and coating (see Fig 2.17).

For most turners, perhaps the most important consideration when choosing abrasives is the type of abrasive material. The most common include garnet, which is an orange color, silicon carbide, which is black, and aluminum oxide, which is available in either brown or white. Each material has its own strengths and weaknesses. An excellent choice is white

FIG 2.17 *An assortment of common abrasives used in pen-making.*

aluminum oxide. This is due more to the color of the abrasive than to its sanding qualities. While sanding, small particles of abrasive grit commonly break away from the paper and become lodged in the pores of the wood. This is of particular concern when sanding woods that are very porous or light in color. Dark-colored abrasives tend to discolor such woods. The white grit of aluminum oxide minimizes discoloration that may occur during sanding.

Backings for abrasives are most commonly made from paper, cloth, or a combination of the two. Cloth-backed abrasives are generally designed to fit machines, such as hand belt sanders and large sanding machines. While cloth backing is very durable and holds up longer than paper, this is usually not a significant advantage to the woodturner because woodturning tends to wear out or clog the abrasive grit long before the backing begins to deteriorate. For most woodturning purposes, paper-backed abrasive is

sufficient and is generally less expensive. The weight of the backing is indicated by a letter. For paper, 'A' weight is very light, 'C' and 'D' are intermediate, and 'E' is heavy. In cloth backing, 'J' is lightweight and flexible, while 'X' is thick and durable. For lathe work, flexible backing is better for forming to curved shapes. Stiff backing will sand flat surfaces better and last longer.

If a waterproof adhesive is used to bond the abrasive grit to the backing, the abrasive will be designated as 'wet/dry'. Wet/dry abrasives allow for water and other liquids to be used as a lubricant during the sanding process. This is usually not an important consideration for woodturners. However, it can be an advantage when sanding pens made of Corian and other synthetics.

Coating refers to the spacing of abrasive grains. When the abrasive grains entirely cover the backing, the coating is referred to as 'closed coat'. Closed-coat abrasives are generally designed for production work on clean surfaces. With 'open-coat' abrasives, only 50 to 70 per cent of the backing surface is covered with abrasive grain. This is best suited for sanding soft, green (wet), or gummy woods, since the abrasive does not become clogged nearly as quickly.

All of the various abrasive materials are available in a range of grit sizes. Low numbers designate coarse grit, while higher numbers indicate the finer grits. For most turning purposes, we recommend use of a medium-weight, white silicone carbide paper in the following grits: 100, 120, 150, 180, 220, 320 and 400. You will find that when turning, some woods will cut much cleaner than others. Having a wide range of grits to select from will allow you to choose the one best suited for the quality of surface you are sanding. The intention, of course, is to begin with the finest grit that will efficiently remove any tool marks or torn grain, and then progress quickly through the higher grits until no sand lines are visible on the surface of the wood.

Micro-Mesh is a new cushioned abrasive product that produces a very fine and uniform scratch pattern (see Fig 2.18). Unlike common sandpaper where the abrasive grit is locked at irregular heights and at random angles, Micro-Mesh incorporates a cushioned action that allows the abrasive grit to move and depress to a common level. As the cushioned abrasive is moved across the surface, the abrasive granules flex and rotate slightly to cut with a smooth shaving action. This results in the ability to produce a highly refined surface in fewer steps. Additional information regarding the use of Micro-Mesh is included in Tips and Tricks (see pages 127–128).

FINISHES

In the general field of woodworking, it is likely that there is no subject about which there is a wider variety of views than that of finishing. If someone were to survey 12 different woodworkers to determine their favorite wood finish, they would probably get a dozen different responses. It seems that every craftsman has devised their own favorite procedure or concocted their own special brew of home-made finish. This may be true also of pen-makers, although there are clearly a few over-the-counter favorites.

In selecting a finish, there are a few qualities of particular interest. First, the finish should highlight the natural beauty of the wood. Second, since pens are often made as a production item, the finish should build to a gloss quickly and dry quickly. The finish should also be appropriate for handling and everyday use.

Probably the most common finish used on pens and small mandrel projects is a thin padding lacquer, often sold as a 'French polish', although it does not consist of the traditional formula. It is applied with a fast buffing motion similar to traditional French polish, and can be worked to a low or very high sheen. A high gloss can also be cut back easily with 0000 steel wool and it can be topped with a coat of paste wax or stick if desired. French polish is popular because of its ease of application, fast drying time, and relative durability. While it is very thin and does not contain enough solids to fill pores and build a gloss on softer woods, this is not usually a concern for pen-makers, since softer woods are generally not used in making pens (see Fig 2.19).

FIG 2.18 *Samples of Micro-Mesh abrasive ranging from 1800 grit to 12000 grit.*

Mylands Friction Polish is rapidly gaining popularity as a preferred finish for pens. The application is similar to that of French polish. However, Mylands Friction Polish builds even faster, resulting in less time being required to achieve a finish coat with good depth.

For open-grain woods Mylands supplies a cellulose sanding sealer. Two quick coats of this sealer, applied while the lathe is switched off, with light sanding in between, will seal the pores allowing the top coat to build more efficiently. Mylands also recommends that the friction polish be sealed in by using an application of carnauba stick wax.

Stick wax is another common finish used on pens. It is a hard, carnauba-based wax. Stick wax is applied to the rotating wood with firm pressure. Heat from friction helps the wax fill the wood pores. Once applied the wax is then buffed with a cloth.

Like friction polish, stick wax is also a quick finish to apply though it does not give the appearance of a built-up finish as much as French polish and friction polish do. While it seems to be less durable than French polish, it has the advantage of being restored more easily with buffing.

A modification of stick wax is the abrasive wax stick produced by Hut Products. Hut stick wax is a combination of natural waxes and polishing compounds that can be used as a finish for stabilized wood, Dymondwood and synthetic materials. It can also be used as a top coat over French polish.

Paste wax is also used as a finish for pens, although it is usually used as a top coat over a previously applied finish. Paste wax is applied to the rotating work with a soft cloth. It generally results in a soft luster. Used alone, it gives a soft finish that provides very little protection. We recommend it as a top coat and for restoring other finishes dulled by use.

While not marketed as such, cyanoacrylate (superglue) is an excellent finish for pens and similar small turnings. It is particularly useful in filling porous materials such as spalted wood and antler. It can be applied by first saturating a cotton swab tip with thin cyanoacrylate and applying the glue to the work while the lathe is not running. The thin formula will be carried by capillary action into the pores of the material. After using the thin formula to penetrate the pores, follow quickly with a

FIG 2.19 French polish, Mylands Friction Polish, stick wax, paste wax and plastic polish are all finishes commonly used to finish different types of pen materials.

similar application of thick or gap-filling cyanoacrylate, then cure the adhesive with a light spray of accelerator. This usually results in a build-up on the surface that must be turned away before sanding.

The final finish is durable, resistant to oils and moisture, and can be buffed to a high gloss if desired. A cyanoacrylate finish is more durable than any of the other finishes discussed here but has the two disadvantages of being relatively costly to purchase, and time-consuming to apply. Care should be taken to ensure that it is not applied to a rotating spindle. Eye protection should also be worn whenever working with cyanoacrylate adhesives.

Plastic polish is recommended for finishing synthetic materials such as Corian and Crushed Velvet. It is also ideal for finishing natural talc and antler. It contains a very fine abrasive that removes fine scratches as it polishes. It is applied with a soft cloth to the rotating piece and will give a satin to moderately high sheen.

The sheen on any of the finishes mentioned can be increased by buffing with a buffing wheel and a touch of jeweler's rouge or other buffing compound. Buffing wheels are available commercially as a lathe accessory that can be mounted on a morse taper and driven by the lathe. They can also be mounted in a drill press. Buffing works particularly well on synthetic materials, Dymondwood and antler (see Fig 2.20).

Selecting a Supplier

When you decide to take the plunge into pen-making, there are many things to consider. Take some time to evaluate what you would like to accomplish with pen-making. Ask yourself if you are making pens for personal use, business or pleasure. Would you like to make other pen-related items like magnifying glasses, key rings or letter openers? What kind of pens would you like to make? How many and what

FIG 2.20   *A buffing wheel can be used to produce a very fine gloss.*

styles of pen are you most interested in? What tools do you have available to make the pens? All these factors will influence what tools and supplies you may need to purchase. Whatever the case, remember that very few people make just one pen.

Whether you are planning to make just a few pens or hundreds, one of the most important things to choose is a good supplier. Your choice of supplier will affect the quality of your pen mechanisms, the variety of pens you have to select from, the quality and availability of accessories, the types of wood and other materials available, and the kind of service you will receive as a customer. When selecting a supplier, do some homework. Consider both quality and selection. Below are a few things to look for when selecting a supplier:

- variety of ballpoint pens, fountain pens and rollerball pens
- lathes, both large and small
- turning-related tools and accessories
- finishing and sanding supplies
- pen-making materials such as wood, synthetics, antler and stabilized woods
- pen display cases and gift boxes
- availability of related projects
- qualified technical service

FIG 2.21 *Starter kits generally include pen kits, pen blanks, a mandrel system, the appropriate bushings and drill bit, a good adhesive and a finish.*

We recommend that you choose a supplier that carries a large range of supplies and has a good reputation. Since there are many projects such as letter openers, magnifying glasses and key chains that can be made using pen mandrels, we suggest you also consider the availability of related projects and accessories. While most beginners will find what they need from one good supplier, the professional may use one main supplier along with several smaller suppliers, to meet a broader range of needs.

STARTER KITS

Most pen suppliers offer a starter kit. These kits take most of the guesswork out of the initial buying process. Kits offer an excellent way to get started in pen-making (see Fig 2.21). Components for starter kits are generally selected and packaged by the retail supplier. With the exception of the machines and basic tools needed, most

starter kits include all the items required to get started making pens. The package is usually priced lower than if the items were sold individually. We view a barrel trimmer as an essential item and suggest you buy one if there is not one included in your starter kit.

We have divided the starter kits into two categories. The first being the beginners kit, for those getting started who would make between 2 and 50 pens per year. The second kit is for professionals who plan to produce more than 50 pens.

THE BEGINNER KITS

Most pen suppliers offer a starter kit which includes approximately five basic pens, the required drill bit, bushings, and basic instructions. More complete beginner kits will vary depending on the supplier and may include mandrels, a barrel trimmer, glue, finish, and wood. The lathe and turning tools are not included in these kits.

THE PROFESSIONAL KITS

Some pen suppliers offer a professional package which is sold with a lathe and tooling. The lathes supplied with these kits are usually mini wood lathes or mini metal lathes. Also included are five or more basic pen kits, required drill bits, bushings, mandrels, a barrel trimmer, glue, finish, wood pen blanks, and basic instructions.

METAL PLATINGS

There are a number of platings available for the metal components of pens (see Fig 2.22). These platings vary in color, finish, durability and cost. It should be noted that the cost difference between most similar types of pen kits are primarily due to the type, quality and thickness of the plating, not to differences in the machining of parts. Most similar pen kits are identical other than the surface plating. We have worked with several types of metal platings, including bright 24 karat gold, bright 10 karat gold, bright cobalt gold, bright titanium gold, satin gold, chrome, satin chrome, satin silver and satin nickel. While we make no claims to being experts in metallurgy, we can provide some observations based on several years' experience of making and using pens with various types of platings.

ECONOMY PLATINGS

The bright, thin-plated, 24 karat gold is often the plating that turners first experience when beginning to make pens because it is the least expensive and is often included in beginner pen kits. Because of the relatively low cost it may be seen as good value, however, the plating is very thin and with regular daily use will begin to wear off in a matter of months or even weeks. For custom-turned pens made from carefully selected woods, we recommend spending a little more money to purchase a pen plating that will offer a longer life.

GOLD ALLOY PLATINGS

The thicker, gold alloy platings offer an excellent balance between cost and durability. Alloy plating combines gold with other metals such as nickel or cobalt that provide much better resistance to wear when compared with pure 24 karat gold plating. These kits are generally offered as either 'cobalt gold' or '10k gold'. The color may be slightly less golden than the 24 karat gold, but the difference is subtle and generally not recognized. Alloy platings are slightly more expensive than 24 karat gold, but are well worth the difference. We recommend these alloy platings as the best overall value for most applications where a bright gold finish is desired.

FIG 2.22   *A sampling of various metal platings used for pens. From left to right: bright gold, satin gold, satin nickel, chrome.*

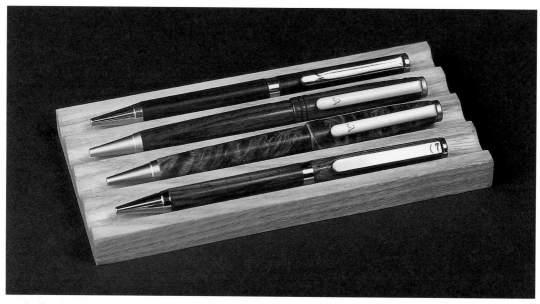

FIG 2.23 *Pens made from kits with four different metal platings. From top to bottom: bright alloy gold, satin gold, satin nickel, bright chrome.*

GOLD TITANIUM PLATINGS

For those who desire a bright gold finish that is extremely resistant to wear, there is gold titanium plating. This plating offers the rich color of 24 karat gold combined with the durability of titanium. Pen kits with titanium plating generally retail for two or three times the price of standard 24k and 10k gold kits. Most suppliers offer a lifetime guarantee on pen kits with titanium plating.

CHROME PLATING

Bright chrome plating is perhaps the most durable when compared with the other platings discussed, with the exception of titanium. It is generally priced about the same as alloy gold platings. Chrome is excellent value when considering cost and durability. It looks very striking combined with some woods such as cocobolo or a good piece of spalted English beech. However, chrome-plated pen kits have not been a large seller. As a result, many suppliers do not offer pen kits in chrome.

SATIN FINISHES

The satin finishes are relatively new on the market and do not yet have the extended track record of the other finishes we have discussed. However, based on information we have been able to obtain from the manufacturers, and from our own use of pens with these platings, we would compare the durability of satin finishes with that of the alloy platings.

Satin finishes offer a soft look that is complemented by the warmth of wood. They not only provide good durability, but also offer some welcome variety to the bright finishes that have long been available (see Fig 2.23).

Satin finishes are currently available in gold and nickel. The satin nickel has a tinge of brown color that tends to bring out the earthy colors that are common to most natural woods.

Satin chrome and satin silver have been provided to us only as prototypes and are currently not widely available.

CHAPTER 3

BASIC PENS AND PENCILS IN DETAIL

FIG 3.1 *Pen blanks with finished pens and pencils.*

STRAIGHT-BARRELED PENS AND PENCILS

The straight-barreled twist pen is the most popular pen style and is excellent for learning pen-making techniques (see Fig 3.1). Straight-barreled twist pens and pencils are relatively quick and easy to produce, and getting started requires a minimal financial investment.

CUTTING THE BLANK

Blanks for twist pens should be cut to approximately $9/16$in (14mm) square by at least $4^5/8$in (118mm) long – i.e. $9/16$ x $9/16$ x $4^5/8$in (14 x 14 x 118mm). This can be accomplished using a variety of methods. Stock that is large enough to handle safely and that has at least one flat face and one flat edge can be ripped to width using a table saw. This method is fast and yields

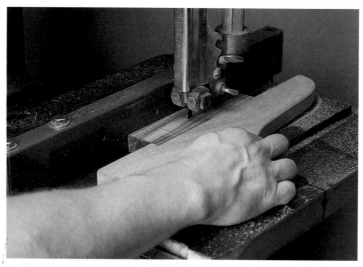

FIG 3.2 *Ripping a pen blank on a bandsaw.*

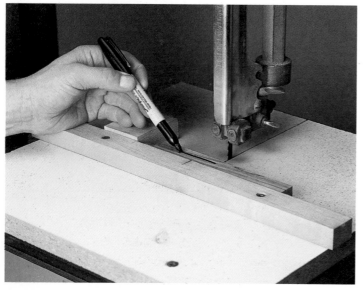

FIG 3.3 *The sliding table with a marked pen blank in position prior to cutting to separate the two halves.*

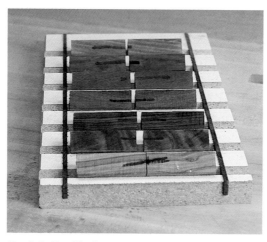

FIG 3.4 *Pen blanks on a storage tray.*

blanks with flat, clean surfaces. For small stock, or stock with irregular surfaces, it is safer and more efficient to rip using a bandsaw (see Fig 3.2).

One feature of a quality hand-turned pen is the grain match between the two halves. Achieving this grain match does not happen by accident, but is the product of taking deliberate steps throughout the process of making the pen. The first of these steps takes place at this point. Once the blanks are ripped to $9/16$in (14mm) square, they should be marked with a strong, visible line extending about an inch (25mm) beyond where the cut will be made to separate the two halves of the pen blank (see Fig 3.3). After the blank is cut into two pieces, the grain can easily be matched by lining up the marked lines. The two pieces for each pen can then be kept as a set, either on a storage tray or bound together with a rubber band or masking tape (see Fig 3.4). After completing each step throughout the process, keep the two halves of each pen blank together as a set.

After the stock is ripped into strips about $9/16$in (14mm) square, the blanks should then be crosscut into lengths of $2^1/4$in (57mm). Two lengths of $2^1/4$in (57mm) will yield one pen or pencil. Crosscutting to length can be accomplished on a bandsaw by simply using a ripping fence as a stop and making the cut freehand. For more control and increased safety, a sliding table with a stop can be made relatively easily. Instructions for making the sliding table are covered in the Tips and Tricks chapter (see pages 110–111).

DRILLING THE BLANK

The wood can now be drilled to receive the brass tube. There are several different drill designs available, each having advantages and disadvantages. Here we will use a basic 7mm brad point twist drill. After mounting the drill bit in the drill press, check with a

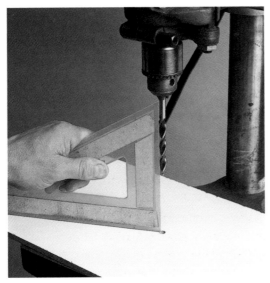

FIG 3.5 *Checking the angle of the drill bit to the table with a small square.*

FIG 3.6 *Drilling using a 'Quick-Grip' clamp to secure the stock.*

small square to assure that the bit is at a right angle to the table (see Fig 3.5). Also set the drill depth gage to stop at the correct depth.

A variety of methods can be used to hold the wood at a right angle to the table during drilling. Regardless of which holding method is used, the drill bit should be centered on the pen blank and the marked (grain match) end of the blank should be in the up position. This way you are assured that even if the drill bit wanders off center while drilling, the holes at the grain match ends will be properly aligned, resulting in a good grain match between the two halves of the pen.

The simplest method is to secure the wood in a small vise or clamp and then drill using a drill press. In Fig 3.6, wood jaws have been secured to the clamp using double-sided tape. The wood jaws are sufficiently large to provide a solid base during drilling. This helps to hold the pen blank square to the table, thus preventing the drilling of an angled hole that may run out through the side of the pen blank (see Fig 3.6).

Drilling will be faster if the rpm is kept relatively high, between 2,000 and 3,000rpm. The feed rate will be determined by how the wood responds to being drilled. This varies

greatly between species. Generally, the feed rate is as aggressive as the wood will allow. The drill bit should be retracted after drilling each 1/2–1in (13–25mm) of increased depth. This reduces the problem of chips compacting in the flutes of the bit and causing excess heat build-up.

There are a few problems inherent to drilling pen blanks, as this requires drilling a deep hole and leaving only a thin section of wood. These problems include heat build-up, the drill bit wandering, and the flutes of the drill bit becoming packed with shavings. Solutions to these problems are discussed in Tips and Tricks (see pages 114–116).

GLUING IN THE BRASS TUBE

Several adhesives provide options for gluing the brass tube in the pen blank. These include gap-filling cyanoacrylate, epoxy, urethane glue and others. Each of these adhesives have two qualities in common. One is that they will bond with metal, not just wood. The other is that they are thick enough to bridge small gaps that may exist between the two surfaces. Here we use gap-filling cyanoacrylate (CA).

FIG 3.7 *Using a plastic straw to apply the glue inside the drilled hole.*

FIG 3.8 *Applying glue using a simple v-cut gluing fixture.*

apply a light coat inside the hole (see Fig 3.7). The brass tube can be lined by rolling the tube in the adhesive. Glue will be conserved if it is contained in a small 'v' or cove cut into a piece of wood (see Fig 3.8).

Once the adhesive has been applied to each piece, push the tube into the wood blank, rotating the tube in a spiral motion as it is being forced in. This further helps to distribute the glue evenly between the tube and the drilled blank.

Pressing the tube in the blank must be done quickly, since CA adhesive sets almost immediately. When pressing the tube into the blank, begin at the grain match end of each piece. This reduces the amount of wood that needs to be removed from the grain match end of each tube when the tube and wood are trimmed flush, thus resulting in the best possible grain match (see Fig 3.9).

After gluing, cure the glue with a spray of accelerator (see Fig 3.10), or set the blanks aside on waxed paper and allow them to cure gradually.

CLEANING AND TRIMMING

Before the pen blank is mounted on the lathe for turning, the inside of the tube must be cleaned of excess glue and each end trimmed so it is clean and square to the ends of the brass tube. The best way to do this is with a barrel trimmer. This tool accomplishes both these tasks simultaneously, as the flute on the shaft

The best results are achieved when glue is applied to both the outside of the brass tube and the inside of the drilled hole. Glue can be applied to the inside of the hole using a foam-tipped make-up brush, a small dowel, or a plastic drinking straw. Dip the applicator in a puddle of glue and simply

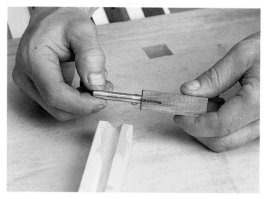

FIG 3.9 *Pressing the tube into the blank.*

FIG 3.10 *Spraying the glue with accelerator.*

FIG 3.11 *Barrel trimming in a bench vise.*

FIG 3.12 *Marking the inside of the tube with a bold marker.*

cleans the inside of the tube while the mill head trims the end true.

The pen blank is held firmly while the barrel trimmer is inserted into the tube and rotated. This can be done using a variety of methods. One method which can be a bit tempting is to hold the blank by hand. This is unsafe, however, and is not a good option, even if wearing gloves. Figure 3.11 shows the pen blank being held in a bench vise. Grip the barrel trimmer in the chuck of a power hand drill and feed the rotating trimmer into the tube until a brass curl is produced (see Fig 3.11). Take care not to be over-aggressive while trimming. This can result in the length of the brass tube being decreased significantly, which may interfere with the function of the pen mechanism.

Before proceeding, a simple step taken here to assure grain match may save some frustration later on. Up to this point, you have maintained grain match based on the line marked on the outside of the wood blanks. When the blanks are turned to a cylinder, this line will be removed and the grain match reference lost. A new reference can be added here by marking the inside of each tube at the grain match end. A bold felt-tip marker works well here (see Fig 3.12), or they may be marked with a scratch awl.

FIG 3.13 *Mandrel with the pen blank and bushings.*

MOUNTING THE BLANK

There are many types of pen mandrel systems available to woodturners. Whether used in a drill chuck or with a morse taper, all mandrel systems require a revolving tail center. In Fig 3.13 we used a double mandrel secured in a morse taper. The morse taper mandrel system consists of a morse taper arbor, a steel mandrel that will hold two barrels at a time, bushings and a tightening nut. The bushings provide a diameter gage for the turner to use to determine the finished outside diameter of the wood. If each end of the wood cylinders is turned to the diameter of the bushings, there will be a smooth transition from the wood to the metal parts of the pen.

The pen blank should be mounted on the double mandrel with at least one bushing at each end and one bushing between the two halves of the pen blank. Take care to line up the grain match marks (see Fig 3.13). The nut should hold all pieces on the mandrel firmly in place. Avoid over-tightening the nut or the tailstock, as this may cause the mandrel not to run true.

TURNING THE PEN

Preferred tools for pen-turning will vary from person to person. We recommend using a small roughing gouge for removing the bulk of the wood (see Fig 3.14). These are aggressive cuts for the purpose of

FIG 3.14 *Turning with a gouge.*

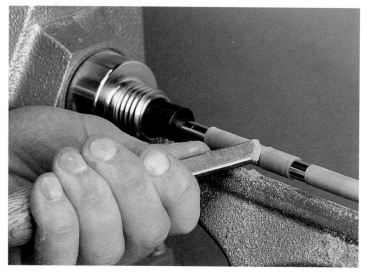

FIG 3.15 *Turning with the heel of a skew.*

quickly bringing the stock to round and removing the excess wood. By cutting from large diameter to small diameter, you will reduce tearout.

Make the finishing cuts with a 1/2in (13mm) skew. The skew can be used either by leading with the toe (long point) or the heel (short point) (see Fig 3.15). We recommend a high lathe speed of between 3,000 and 3,500rpm. This allows the turner to be more aggressive and speeds up the process of both turning and finishing.

SANDING AND FINISHING

With a good sharp edge and proper tool use, the surface should be cut fairly clean and require minimal sanding. Sanding and finishing can be accomplished quickly, the whole process generally taking less than a minute or two. Have on hand abrasive paper starting at 120 grit and progressing to 180, 220 and finally 320 or 400.

Start sanding with 120 grit, or finer if the cut is sufficiently clean. With the lathe spinning, hold the abrasive paper against the wood, apply a medium amount of pressure and move the paper quickly from end to end (see Fig 3.16). When all tool marks and torn grain are removed, progress to the next, finer grit and repeat the process. After sanding with 320 grit, turn the lathe off and while rotating the spindle slowly by hand, sand lengthwise with the grain using 320 or 400 grit. This will remove cross-grain circular scratches.

Several finishes may be selected for use on a pen or pencil. Padding lacquer (French polish) is a finish that is commonly used because of its ease of application, quick drying time and the possibilities it allows for adjusting the sheen. The first coat should be applied with the lathe stopped (see Fig 3.17). This allows the finish to penetrate into the open pores of the wood, rather than glaze over them and trap sanding dust, thus leaving the pores as light-colored specks.

A moderate amount of finish should be placed on a lint-free cloth. Apply the first coat by rotating the spindle by hand and moving the rag quickly along the wood. Then turn the lathe on and continue the process (see Fig 3.18). The high speed of the lathe and a little hand pressure will produce heat which helps the finish build and cure faster. Keep the rag moving constantly.

Once the desired sheen is produced, the finish can be topped off with a light coat of wax. For a softer luster, apply 0000 steel wool lengthwise with the grain while the lathe is off, then top with a coat of wax. After use, a light coat of wax applied with a cloth will quickly restore the soft luster.

ASSEMBLING THE PEN

Assembly is the final step that will complete the pen. Several methods can be used to press the pen parts together. In this chapter we will use a bench vise. The vise should have wood jaws, as metal jaws can easily damage the wood barrel as well as the plating on the pen mechanism.

Before beginning assembly, carefully read the assembly instructions provided by the supplier. Assembly procedures vary with the different types of pens. Once you are familiar with the assembly process you may consider making some simple jigs or fixtures to increase efficiency. This is strongly recommended if you are making large quantities of pens or pencils.

Prior to assembly, the sharp corners on each end of the wood barrels should be sanded slightly. This makes for a smoother transition between the wood and metal components of the pen. To accomplish this, hold the barrel at approximately 45° to a piece of fine abrasive paper, and rotate the barrel while dragging it across the surface (see Fig 3.19).

The procedure for making pens and pencils is identical until you get to the point of assembly. To assemble a pen, first lay out

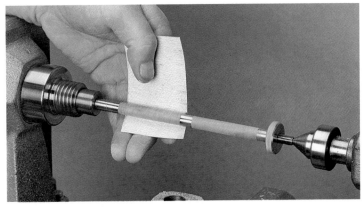

FIG 3.16 *Sanding can be accomplished quickly.*

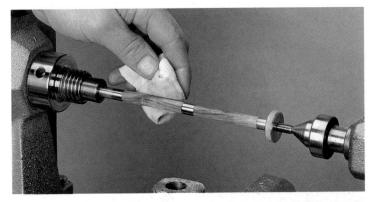

FIG 3.17 *Applying the first coat of French polish with the lathe stopped.*

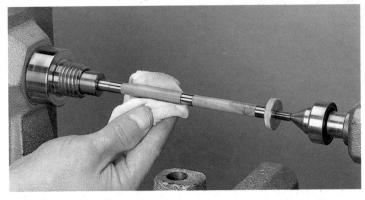

FIG 3.18 *Applying the final finishing coat with the lathe power on.*

FIG 3.19 *Softening the edge of the wood barrel by hand-sanding.*

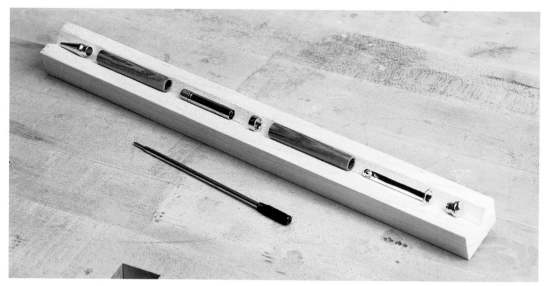

FIG 3.20 *The components of a twist pen prior to assembly.*

the parts according to the drawings provided by the supplier. Remember to keep the grain match between the two wood cylinders by looking for the marks on the inside of the tubes. The marked ends should be placed toward the center of the pen. A small board with a shallow v-cut helps keep the parts from rolling out of position (see Fig 3.20).

Place the writing tip of the pen into the non-grain match end of one of the tubes. Press the two together in a bench vise (see Fig 3.21). Next, press the pen transmission, brass end first, into the grain match end of the same tube. There is an indentation ring on the chrome portion of the transmission that indicates approximately how far the transmission should be pressed in. The exact position of the transmission will vary somewhat depending on the length of the tubes, which may be slightly different due to the trimming process. To check this, position the ink cartridge and fully extend the ballpoint tip. If it does not extend far enough, remove the cartridge, press the transmission further into the tube, then check again. If it extends too far, the pen will have to be disassembled. This process, requiring special tools, is covered in Tips and Tricks (see pages 131–132).

FIG 3.21 *Pressing the tip into the tube.*

FIG 3.22 *Pressing the transmission in while using a v-stop block to achieve the proper depth.*

FIG 3.23 *Pressing the clip and cap into the tube.*

A simple fixture that takes the guesswork out of this process is a v-block cut to the length of $3^{11}/_{32}$in (85mm). The 'v' helps to hold the parts in position while the ends of the block stop the vise at the correct depth (see Fig 3.22). The brass ring is placed around the exposed end of the transmission, separating the two tubes.

Now install the clip and cap. To do this, insert the cap into the clip ring, position these at the non-grain match end of the second barrel, and start to push the cap into the barrel with hand pressure. Then press the parts together in the vise (see Fig 3.23).

The final step is to slide the tube containing the clip onto the exposed transmission. The pen is now assembled and the barrels can be rotated to align the grain match. Generally, the grain match is aligned when the pen is in the retracted position (see Fig 3.24).

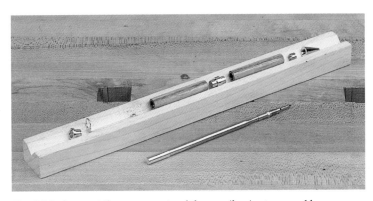

FIG 3.25 *Lay out the components of the pencil prior to assembly.*

FIG 3.26 *Pressing the clip into position.*

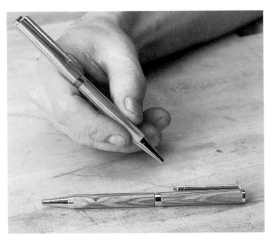

FIG 3.24 *The completed pen showing the grain match.*

FIG 3.27 *Pressing the tip bushing into position.*

ASSEMBLING THE PENCIL

Pencil assembly requires a slightly different procedure than that followed when assembling pens. As with pen assembly, first read the supplier's instructions and lay out the pencil parts as directed (see Fig 3.25).

First press the clip into the non-grain match end of one barrel (see Fig 3.26), then press one end of the connecting coupler into the other end of the same barrel. Next, press

the stepped end of the tip bushing into the non-grain match end of the second barrel (see Fig 3.27). Now the two barrels can be pressed together onto the connecting coupler.

Since grain match cannot be adjusted after assembly, the grain match between the two barrels must be aligned carefully at this point. This process can be simplified by the use of a simple fixture that holds all the pieces in alignment. The fixture consists of two blocks of wood with a groove cut in

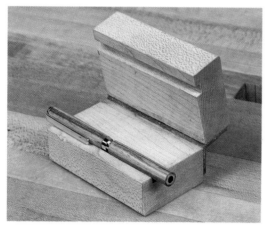

FIG 3.28 *The pencil assembly fixture helps achieve good grain alignment.*

FIG 3.29 *Using the pencil assembly fixture to keep the pencil components in the correct position while pressing them together.*

FIG 3.30 *Connecting the writing tip.*

each block (see Fig 3.28). The two blocks are held together by a stiff leather hinge which holds the fixture in an open position when no pressure is applied. The pencil parts are gripped by hand pressure between the two jaws of the fixture while the pencil is pressed together in a bench vise (see Fig 3.29).

Finally, the pencil mechanism is inserted through the clip end of the pencil and screwed onto the writing tip (see Fig 3.30). To extend the pencil lead, press several times with your thumb on the pencil plunger. To retract the lead, hold the plunger down and push the lead back into the pencil (see Fig 3.31).

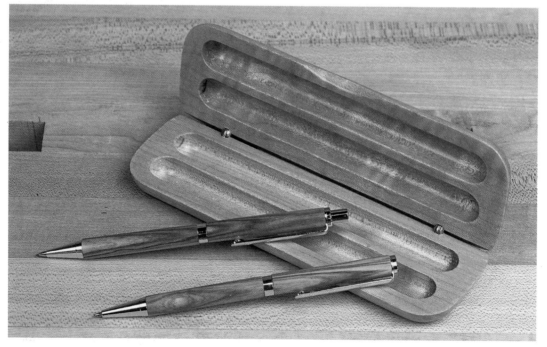

FIG 3.31 *The completed pen and pencil set.*

CHAPTER 4

EUROPEAN AND AMERICAN STYLE PENS

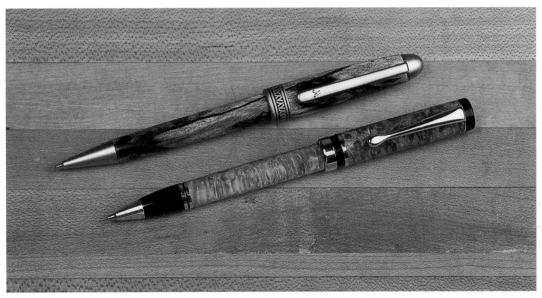

FIG 4.1 *European and American style pens.*

LARGE-BARRELED PENS

Large-barreled ballpoint pens have a rich history dating back some fifty years. The Parker pen company of America and the Mont Blanc pen company of Germany have developed many lines of pens and have been leaders in the pen-making industry for many years. Some of the more popular styles of pens developed by these companies have become well known and easily recognized for distinctive design features such as the shape of the pen body, a particular style of clip, or a specific logo.

The pens covered in this chapter are designed after two of the most popular pens produced by the Parker and Mont Blanc pen manufacturers. We will refer to the two styles of pen by the continent of the pen company – American for the Parker style pen and European for the Mont Blanc style. It should be noted that the mechanisms for these pens are not manufactured by Parker and Mont Blanc and should not be referred to as a 'Parker' pen or a 'Mont Blanc' pen.

In addition to the distinctive shape offered by these styles of pen, the larger diameter pens are also superior for showing off the grain in a special piece of wood.

We have included both the American and European style pens in this chapter because the processes for preparing the stock and turning the pens are very similar. The primary differences between these two

FIG 4.2   American and European pen and pencil in wood display boxes.

pens are found in the parts that make up the kits and variations in the assembly process.

Kits for matching pencils are also available for both styles. These also differ somewhat in the internal parts and assembly process, but the turning processes are similar (see Fig 4.2). The assembly process for each pen differs somewhat and is covered separately.

USING STABILIZED WOOD

Most pen suppliers offer a broad selection of stabilized woods (see Fig 4.3). Stabilized woods have been impregnated with a plastic resin. The result is a wood/plastic composite that provides a number of distinct advantages – increased density, improved working properties, better resistance to moisture and better wear resistance. Once stabilized, spalted English beech is one of the finest woods available for pens. While the working properties of stabilized woods are quite similar to those of dense hardwoods, there are some differences. More information regarding stabilized woods is included in Chapter 8, Alternative Materials (see pages 93–94).

CUTTING THE BLANK

Blanks for the American and European style ballpoint pens should be approximately ³⁄₄in (19mm) square by at least 5in (127mm) long – i.e. ³⁄₄ x ³⁄₄ x 5in (19 x 19 x 127mm). Stabilized pen blanks are generally pre-cut to rough dimensions before being treated.

Mark a bold visible line extending about an inch (25mm) beyond where the cut will be made to separate the two halves of the pen blank. After the stock is marked, measure the tube lengths in the kit for the type of pen you are producing. These

FIG 4.3   Stabilized wood pen blanks.

measurements will vary according to the supplier and the style of pen.

The blank should then be crosscut into two lengths, one for the upper tube and one for the lower tube. Crosscutting to length can be accomplished using a variety of different methods. One very simple way is to cut the blank freehand. In the method shown here, masking tape is set into position on the bandsaw table to indicate the proper length of the long and short sections needed for the European style pen (see Fig 4.4). When crosscutting the blank, be sure to have the blade guard in position and take care to keep your hands well away from the blade (see Fig 4.5).

After the blank has been cut into two, the grain can easily be matched by lining up the marked lines on each. The two pieces for each pen should then be kept together as a set (see Fig 4.6).

DRILLING THE BLANK

The wood can now be drilled to receive the brass tube. We suggest that when buying your pen kits you also purchase the drill bit that is recommended by the supplier. Many of the kits require drill bit sizes that may otherwise be difficult to find. Pen kits may require bits that are either standard, metric or letter size. By purchasing the drill bits that have been recommended by the supplier, you will be buying bits that have been checked by the supplier to guarantee accuracy for drilling. The suppliers should have a good stock of drill bits on hand and can make recommendations for specific use.

There are several methods that can be used to hold the wood in place during drilling. Each half of the pen blank should be drilled with the grain match mark in the up position and with the drill bit centered on the end of the blank. This way, you are assured that even if the drill bit wanders off center while drilling, the holes at the grain match ends will be properly aligned.

FIG 4.4   Masking tape on the bandsaw table indicating what lengths to cut for the long and short tubes.

FIG 4.5   Freehand crosscutting the pen blank on the bandsaw.

FIG 4.6   Cut pen blanks bound together with a rubber band.

FIG 4.7 *Drilling using a gate jig.*

FIG 4.8 *A simple storage tray made using brazing rods to hold both halves of the pen blank.*

One excellent method to secure the wood for drilling is to use a shop-made 'gate jig'. This holds the pen blank securely, square to the table, allows for quick insertion and removal of pen blanks, and provides for easy visual centering of the drill bit on the blank (see Fig 4.7). Instructions for using the gate jig are included in the chapter on Tips and Tricks (see pages 112–113).

When drilling stabilized woods, a high spindle speed of 2,000 to 3,000rpm may be maintained. However, it is usually necessary to reduce the feed rate compared with drilling untreated wood. Feed as aggressively as the stabilized wood will allow – this will vary from piece to piece. The drill bit should be retracted after drilling each $1/2$–1in (13–25mm) of increased depth. This reduces the problem of chips compacting in the flutes of the bit and causing excessive heat build-up, which is even more problematic with stabilized woods than untreated woods. We have found the bullet-style bit to be the best for drilling stabilized woods.

While drilling each blank, remember to ease up on the downward pressure as you near the bottom of the blank. This will reduce the amount of tear-out as the drill protrudes through the bottom end of the blank. For additional drilling information see Tips and Tricks (see pages 114–116).

After drilling, keep both halves of each pen together as sets. One handy method for storing blanks after drilling is a board containing rows of brazing rods or $1/8$in (3mm) dowel rods (see Fig 4.8).

GLUING IN THE BRASS TUBE

In the example shown here we used five-minute epoxy for gluing the brass tubes into the drilled blank. With most brands of five-minute epoxy you will, as the name implies, have about five minutes of working time. The epoxy should be cured and the piece ready to turn in about 30 minutes.

The best results are achieved when glue is applied to both the outside of the brass tube and the inside of the drilled hole. After mixing the epoxy, apply it to the inside of the hole. We use a make-up brush with a foam tip. Dip the brush in a puddle of glue and apply a light coat inside the hole (see Fig 4.9). The brass tube can be lined with epoxy by rolling the tube in the adhesive. Epoxy will be conserved if it is contained in a small 'v' or cove cut into a piece of wood.

Once the adhesive has been applied to each piece, push the tube into the wood blank, rotating the tube in a spiral motion as it is being forced in. This further helps to distribute the glue evenly between the tube and the drilled blank (see Fig 4.10). After gluing in the tubes, place the blanks on waxed paper and allow the epoxy time to cure.

CLEANING AND TRIMMING

Before the pen blank is mounted on the lathe for turning, the inside of the tube must be cleaned of excess glue and each end trimmed so that it is clean and square to the end of the brass tube. The best way to do this is with a barrel trimmer. In order for the barrel trimmer to work with tubes larger in diameter than 7mm, such as the American style pen, you will need to either buy or make an adapter sleeve. An adapter sleeve allows a standard barrel trimmer to be used to trim blanks with tubes larger than 7mm.

FIG 4.9   Using a foam-tipped make-up brush to apply glue inside the drilled hole.

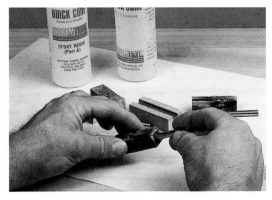

FIG 4.10   Pressing the tube into the drilled hole.

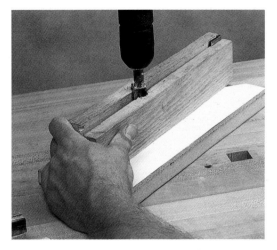

FIG 4.11   Using the gate jig to secure the pen blank while cleaning with the barrel trimmer.

Some suppliers carry metal adapter sleeves. However, there are pens and other mandrel projects that require odd-sized tubes for which adapters are not available. Knowing how to make your own adapter sleeve is a useful technique that will most probably come in handy. For directions on how to make an adapter sleeve, refer to Tips and Tricks (see page 120).

When trimming the 7mm tube for the European style pen, the trimmer can be inserted directly into the tube. However, the larger 'O'-size tube for the American style pen requires the use of an adapter sleeve. The adapter sleeve is inserted into the tube to be trimmed. The pen blank should be held firmly while the barrel trimmer is inserted into the tube and rotated.

The pen blank can be secured using a variety of methods. Here the pen blank is being held in the same gate jig that was used to secure the blank while drilling. Grip the barrel trimmer in the chuck of a power hand drill and feed the rotating trimmer into the tube until a brass curl is produced (see Fig 4.11). Take care to not be over-aggressive while trimming. This can result in the length of the brass tube being decreased significantly, which may interfere with the function of the pen. This is particularly true of the American style pen.

Mounting the Blank

As discussed in Chapter 2, there are many types of pen mandrel system available. In this chapter we will use a one-piece single mandrel secured in a morse taper and revolving tail center. The single mandrel is similar to the double mandrel except that it is shorter and only one half of the pen can be mounted at a time. The shorter mandrel, however, allows the turner to work more aggressively and is less prone to the unwanted flexing that sometimes occurs in the center of the longer double mandrel. This set-up consists of a morse taper arbor, the single mandrel, bushings to fit the pen being made, and a tightening nut.

The pen blank should be mounted on the mandrel with the appropriate bushings at each end of the pen blank. The nut should hold all pieces on the mandrel firmly in place. The blanks should be mounted on the mandrel with the appropriate bushings as referred to in the supplier's instructions. It is the bushing provided by the supplier that will determine the finished outside diameter of the blanks.

Turning

AMERICAN STYLE PEN
To turn the lower blank of the American style pen, mount the blank and the necessary bushings on the mandrel (see Fig 4.13). The American style pen has straight barrels on both the top and bottom sections. With this pen, no curved lines or steps are necessary, so simply turn the wood to the bushing diameter.

Stabilized woods respond well to sanding and require no special procedures beyond those used for untreated woods. However, possible health hazards associated with sanding them are not known. It seems reasonable that the use of a good ventilation system or mask may be even more important when working near the fine dust from stabilized woods than from woods not impregnated with a plastic resin.

Stabilized woods also finish well without any special treatment. Since the wood is saturated with a clear plastic, quite often a good buffing is all that is needed. However, most pen makers prefer to add a finish of some kind. One finish which works very well is thin cyanoacrylate adhesive (CA). Unfortunately, in relation to standard finishes, CA glue has the distinct disadvantage of being relatively expensive. It does, however, result in the most durable finish discussed within the chapters of this book. CA adhesive can be applied to produce a low luster or a very high gloss.

To apply CA glue as a finish, place a drop of thin CA on the tip of a cotton swab. With the lathe off, rotate the spindle by hand while applying the glue to the surface of the barrel (see Fig 4.14). If there are small

FIG 4.13 *The lower section of the pen blank mounted a single mandrel.*

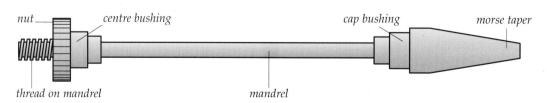

FIG 4.12 *The bushing and mandrel for each blank.*

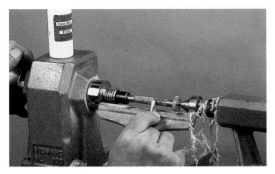

FIG 4.14 *Applying thin CA adhesive as a finish.*

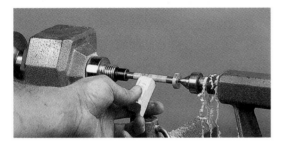

FIG 4.15 *Using Hut pen polish.*

FIG 4.16 *The upper blank with bushings.*

FIG 4.17 *Parting away a section of wood to take the center band.*

FIG 4.18 *The finished blank without the center band, with the brass tube showing where the wood has been removed.*

voids in the wood, which is often the case with burl woods, place a drop of gap-filling CA glue on the same cotton tip and apply in the same manner.

The CA glue generally builds and dries rather quickly. A light shot of CA accelerator will speed the process. Use a mild accelerator which does not force the CA to bubble as it cures. Before turning on the lathe and proceeding to sand, make sure the CA is thoroughly set. We recommend wearing eye protection whenever working with CA adhesives.

Using a fine abrasive grit, sand away any excess CA glue. Complete the sanding process with 0000 steel wool. If a top coat is desired, almost any good wax will do well.

For the pen featured here we applied a top coat of stick wax that was especially formulated for pen finishing, produced by Hut Products. To apply the wax, the stick is held with moderate pressure against the rotating wood (see Fig 4.15). Excess wax is removed with a soft, dry cloth while the blank is rotating.

To turn the upper section of the American style pen, mount the upper blank using the appropriate bushings as shown in Fig 4.16. Refer to the supplier's instructions to ensure that you have the correct set-up (see Fig 4.16). Turn the blank to match the bushing diameters on each end. Sand and finish the top blank at this point.

The pen kit shown here has a center band that will be press fitted onto the brass tube during assembly. This requires that a section of wood $7/32$in (6mm) wide be removed to expose the brass tube. This is best accomplished with a small parting tool cut (see Fig 4.17). Stop the lathe to inspect the shoulder of the cut (see Fig 4.18). If the shoulder is cut cleanly, your pen is now ready to assemble.

EUROPEAN STYLE PEN

When mounted and ready for turning, each section of the European style pen will have two different diameters of bushings (see Fig 4.19). When turning each section of the European style pen, it is necessary to turn a gently curved taper between the two bushings. Turn down to the bushing on each end of the blank with a small gouge, leaving the blank thicker in the middle. Then begin turning the curved taper, cutting 'downhill' from the larger bushing to the smaller bushing (see Fig 4.20).

The roughing cuts can be made with fairly aggressive passes using a gouge. Finishing cuts are generally best made with a skew. This section of the pen is now ready to be sanded and finished. Notice the very subtle final curve and taper of this section of the pen (see Fig 4.21).

The upper portion of the pen requires different bushings from the lower section. To turn the upper portion, mount the upper blank of the pen using the appropriate bushings, including the floating center band bushing as shown in Fig 4.22. Refer to the supplier's instructions in order to ensure that you have the correct set-up (see Fig 4.22).

Turn the blank, leaving it a little larger than the band bushings. Here, we show

FIG 4.21   *The finished, tapered lower section of the European style pen.*

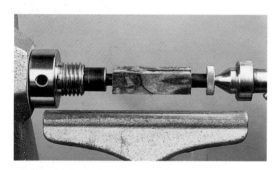

FIG 4.19   *The lower section of the European pen. The right bushing is larger in diameter than the left.*

FIG 4.22   *The upper section of the European pen blank mounted with the necessary bushings.*

FIG 4.20   *Rough turning the slightly curved taper of the European style pen.*

FIG 4.23 *Making finishing cuts with the toe of a skew chisel.*

FIG 4.24 *Turning a short tenon, used to check the fit of the inside diameter of the center band bushing.*

FIG 4.25 *Using a specially ground tool to cut the ³⁄₁₆in (5mm) long tenon.*

finishing cuts being made using a ¹⁄₂in (13mm) skew, leading with the toe of the skew (see Fig 4.23). Next, with a small parting tool, cut a ¹⁄₈in (3mm) long tenon for the center band (see Fig 4.24).

Test the fit of the center band by sliding the band onto the tenon. This will give you the correct diameter of the outside of the tenon. Once the band slides onto the tenon snugly, cut the rest of the length of the tenon making it approximately ³⁄₁₆in (5mm) long. Use of a special tool ground with a ³⁄₁₆in (5mm) wide edge allows you to make this cut for the proper length of the tenon without measuring (see Fig 4.25).

Once you have accomplished the proper fit for the center band, turn the remainder of the blank using the center band bushing and the cap bushing to ensure that the

FIG 4.26 *Finished blank showing the tenon that will receive the center band.*

proper diameters of each end are reached. Now slide the tenon out of the way for the remainder of the turning and sanding. Remember to turn a gentle curve on the cap that will match the curve on the lower blank. You are now ready to sand and finish the blank (see Fig 4.26).

Pre-Assembly

Before beginning assembly, carefully read the instructions provided by the supplier. Assembly procedures often vary with the different styles and makes of pen. Once you are familiar with the assembly process, if you are planning to make large quantities of American or European style pens, you may consider making some simple jigs or fixtures to increase efficiency.

Prior to assembly, the sharp corners on each end of the wood barrels should be sanded lightly. To do this simply hold the corner of the barrel at approximately 45° to the surface of a fine abrasive paper, then rotate and drag the barrel.

FIG 4.27 *The drill can be used as an arbor press for assembling pen parts.*

Final Assembly

EUROPEAN STYLE PEN

For this chapter we used a drill press to assemble the pens (see Fig 4.27). This method is designed to be fast and very accurate. The drill press table provides a flat, horizontal surface that helps keep the pen parts standing upright, which makes assembly easier. Place a scrap of medium-density fiberboard (MDF) on the drill press table and mount a $1/2$ x 3in (13 x 76mm) long bolt in the drill chuck. To protect the pen parts from the head of the bolt, secure a small piece of wood to the head using double-sided tape or thick cyanoacrylate adhesive.

To assemble the pen, first lay out the parts according to the drawings provided by the supplier (see Fig 4.28). Press the tip into the small end of the tapered lower barrel (see Fig 4.29). Next press the twist

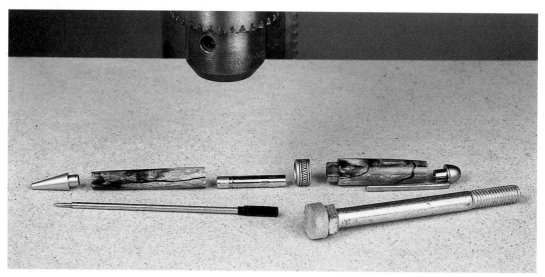

FIG 4.28 *Parts for the European style pen. Also shown is the bolt that will be held in the drill press chuck.*

FIG 4.29 *Pressing the tip into the small end of the lower barrel.*

FIG 4.30 *Pressing the transmission using a press block as a depth stop.*

FIG 4.31 *Pressing the clip/cap assembly into the barrel.*

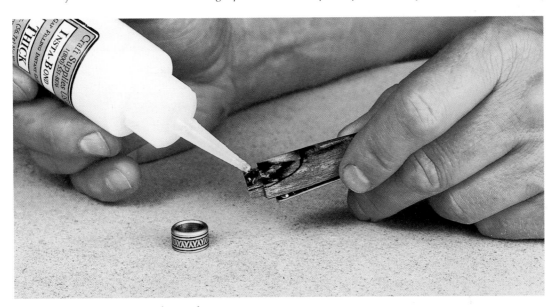

FIG 4.32 *Applying cyanoacrylate to the tenon.*

mechanism, brass end first, into the opposite end of the same tube. Use the press block described in Chapter 3 (see page 37) to set the correct depth of the mechanism (see Fig 4.30).

Pre-assemble the cap and clip by sliding the cap stud through the clip ring hole and screwing it into the cap nut, then press the clip/cap assembly into the top of the upper barrel (see Fig 4.31).

To secure the center band onto the upper blank, place a small amount of gap-filling CA adhesive around the tenon (see Fig 4.32). Rotate the center band as you push it onto the tenon to ensure that the glue is spread evenly around the tenon.

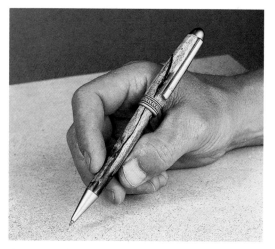

FIG 4.33 *The completed European style pen.*

Finally, insert the refill and slide the upper tube onto the mechanism to complete the pen (see Fig 4.33).

AMERICAN STYLE PEN

To assemble the American style pen, first lay out the parts according to the drawings provided by the supplier (see Fig 4.34). To assemble the lower section of the pen, begin with the pen tip. Push the gold tip into the black center section (see Fig 4.35), then slide the gold ring onto the tenon of the black center section. Next, press the assembled tip into one end of the lower tube (see Fig 4.36).

FIG 4.34 *Parts for the American style pen, and the bolt used for the assembly process.*

FIG 4.35 *Pressing the two metal parts of the tip together.*

FIG 4.36 *Pressing the assembled tip into the lower barrel.*

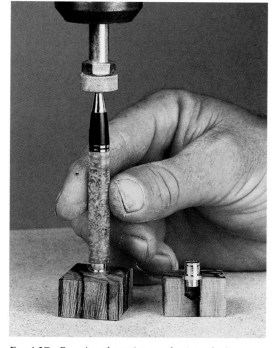

FIG 4.37 *Pressing the twist coupler into the lower tube. The visual aid on the right shows a cut-away section of the coupler in the press block.*

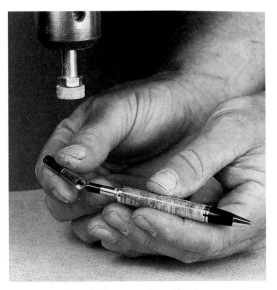

FIG 4.38 *Completing assembly of the lower section.*

FIG 4.39 *Pressing the clip/cap assembly onto the top end of the upper barrel.*

FIG 4.40 *Pressing the center band onto the exposed end of the brass tube.*

Press the smooth end of the twist coupler into the other end of the lower tube.

In order to protect the threads during assembly, a simple press block will need to be made. Start with a small scrap of hardwood about ³/₄in (19mm) thick and 1¹/₂in (38mm) square. Drill a ³/₈in (10mm) deep hole into the press block with a ⁵/₁₆in (8mm) drill. Place the threaded end of the twist coupler into the hole when pressing the smooth end into the lower tube (see Fig 4.37).

Continue by placing the spring over the writing end of the refill, then insert the refill into the lower tube. Complete the lower portion of the pen by screwing the twist mechanism over the refill and onto the twist coupler (see Fig 4.38).

To assemble the upper section of the pen, first pre-assemble the cap and clip by sliding the cap stud through the clip ring hole and screwing it into the cap nut. Then press the clip/cap assembly into the top of the upper barrel (see Fig 4.39).

Next, press the center band onto the exposed end of the brass tube (see Fig 4.40). If this is not a snug press fit, it may require a touch of gap-filling CA glue to secure the center in place. To complete the pen, slide the finished upper barrel onto the twist mechanism (see Fig 4.41).

FIG 4.41 *The completed American style pen.*

CHAPTER 5

TAPERED ROLLERBALL AND FOUNTAIN PENS

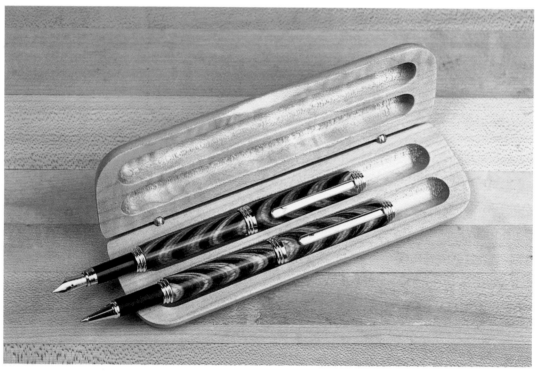

FIG 5.1 Completed tapered rollerball and fountain pens.

CLASSIC SHAPES

Tapered rollerball and fountain pens are designed with a classic look and feel, and they are some of the most exquisite pens that can be produced on the lathe. The tapered curve and long line make them favorites among pen collectors. But all these good looks have a price. The tapered rollerball kits, customized step drills and special bushings are relatively expensive compared with other pens. The process used to make a tapered rollerball is also

somewhat more extensive than that used for the pens covered in previous chapters. We have selected Dymondwood for the two pens featured here.

CUTTING THE BLANK

Blanks for the tapered rollerball and fountain pens should be cut to approximately ³/₄in (19mm) square by at least 5¹/₄in (133mm) long, i.e. ³/₄ x ³/₄ x 5¹/₄in (19 x 19 x 133mm). This can be done in several ways. Perhaps the simplest way is

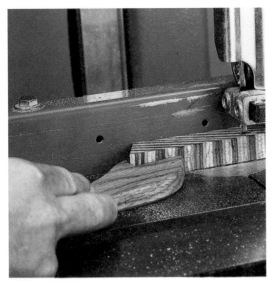

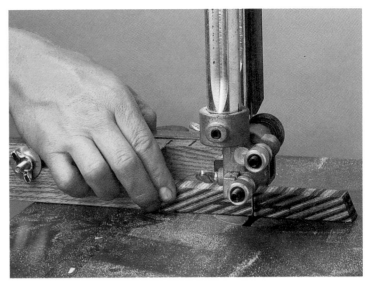

FIG 5.2 *Ripping a pen blank on a bandsaw using a rip fence and a push stick.*

FIG 5.3 *Crosscutting pen blanks to length using a slip fence on a bandsaw.*

to rip the stock on a bandsaw using a rip fence and feed the piece with the aid of a push stick (see Fig 5.2).

Once the blanks are ripped to ³/₄in (19mm) square, they should be marked with a strong visible line, extending about an inch (25mm) beyond where the cut will be made, to separate the two halves of the pen blank. After the stock is marked, the blanks should then be crosscut into lengths that are each about ¹/₁₆in (1–2mm) longer than the brass tubes provided in the pen kit. One way to crosscut the blanks to length is to

use a bandsaw equipped with a miter gage and an auxiliary slip fence – a type of adjustable fence with marks for different lengths of pen blanks. The adjustable slip fence is designed to allow quick-change settings for cutting blanks of different lengths (see Fig 5.3).

After the blank is cut into two pieces, the grain can easily be matched by lining up the marked lines. The two pieces for each pen should then be kept in pairs. One method of keeping the sets together is to wrap them with a bit of masking tape (see Fig 5.4).

FIG 5.4 *The matching blanks for one pen taped together.*

DRILLING THE BLANK

The wood can now be drilled to receive the brass tube. Two different stepped drill bits are required for the tapered rollerball. The step drills are custom-made to match each tube, one for the lower tube and one for the top (see Fig 5.5). Step drills are quite expensive but are well worth the price. Although step drilling can be accomplished using separate standard drill bits, this process is time-consuming and prone to problems. We suggest that you purchase the appropriate step drills when buying your pen kits.

A variety of methods can be used to hold the wood in place during drilling. Regardless of which holding method is used, each half of the pen blank should be drilled with the grain match mark in the up position and the bit centered on the blank. This assures that even if the drill bit does wander off-center while drilling, the holes at the grain match ends will be properly aligned and a good grain match between the halves will be maintained.

One of many methods that can be used to secure the wood while drilling with a drill press is a modified parallel jaw clamp. In Fig 5.6 auxiliary wood jaws have been secured to a parallel jaw clamp using double-sided tape. The auxiliary jaws were previously machined to fit the clamp, including the addition of v-grooves to aid in centering and securing the pen blank. The wood jaws of the clamp are sufficiently large to provide a solid base during drilling. This helps to hold the pen blank square to the table, thus preventing the drilling of an angled hole that may run out through the side of the pen blank (see Fig 5.6).

When drilling Dymondwood with these larger bits, we recommend reducing the drill speed to about 1,500rpm. The feed rate should be adjusted according to how the material responds. This varies greatly between wood species and other types of

FIG 5.5 The step drill and a cross section of a drilled piece of wood showing how the tube fits into the drilled hole.

FIG 5.6 Drilling using a modified parallel jaw clamp.

FIG 5.7 Drilled blanks stored on a board with grooves cut on the table saw.

material. When drilling, the drill bit should be retracted after each ½–1in (13–25mm) of increased depth. This reduces the problem of chips compacting in the flutes of the bit and causing excessive heat build-up. Dymondwood is very sensitive to excess heat, which may cause hairline cracks during the drilling process.

In order to become familiar with the process of step drilling we suggest that you first do a bit of practice by drilling some scrap pen blanks. Use inexpensive wood that is prepared in the same manner as the actual pen blanks. Drill the first test hole only three-quarters of the way through the blank. Stop the drill press and slide your tube into the hole to test the fit. Drill the rest of the way through the blank and test the fit again. The tube should slide into the blank until it rests just under the blank surface. By working out the bugs on a practice pen blank,

you will save that nice, exotic blank for a finished pen rather than for the trash can.

After drilling, continue to keep both halves of each pen blank together as a set (see Fig 5.7).

GLUING IN THE BRASS TUBE

For the project shown here we used a polyurethane adhesive (PU) to glue the stepped brass tubes into the drilled blank. PU adhesive gives plenty of working time and produces an excellent bond. The best results are achieved when glue is applied to both the outside of the brass tube and the inside of the drilled hole. An old screwdriver makes a handy glue applicator. Roll the shaft of the screwdriver in a puddle of glue and apply a light coat inside the hole (see Fig 5.8). The brass tube can be lined with

FIG 5.8 Lining the inside of the hole with glue, using a screwdriver.

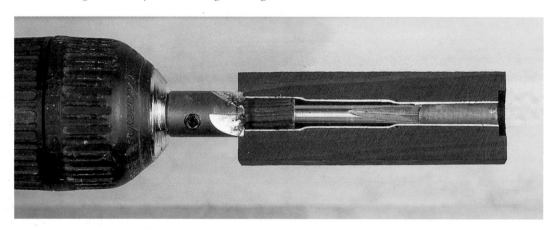

FIG 5.9 A cut-away of the blank, with the tube, wooden adapter and trimmer in place.

glue by rolling it in the adhesive. Glue will be conserved if it is contained in a small 'v' or cove cut into a piece of wood.

Once the adhesive has been applied to each piece, push the tube into the wood blank, rotating the tube in a spiral motion as it is being forced in. This further helps to distribute the glue evenly between the tube and the drilled blank. After gluing in the tubes, place the blank on a piece of waxed paper until the curing process is complete. Ten minutes after gluing, check to see if the tube has crept back out, due to glue or air expansion. If either of the tubes has moved, gently push them back into position. This is particularly important to watch for when using PU glues.

CLEANING AND TRIMMING

Both the tapered rollerball and the fountain pen require a step tube. Since the larger portions of the tubes are wider than 7mm, adapter sleeves are required for the trimming process. Some suppliers carry metal adapter sleeves as a standard item. However, knowing how to make your own adapter sleeve is very useful. In fact, for this particular style of pen, three different adapter sleeves are required. Instructions on how to make an adapter sleeve are included in Tips and Tricks (see page 120).

The adapter sleeve is inserted into the tube to be trimmed (see Fig 5.9). The pen blank should be held firmly while the barrel trimmer is inserted into the tube and rotated. The pen blank can be secured using a variety of different methods. In Fig 5.10 the pen blank is shown being held in the same modified parallel jaw clamp that was used to secure the blank while drilling. Grip the barrel trimmer in the chuck of a power hand drill and feed the rotating trimmer into the tube until a brass curl is produced (see Fig 5.10).

MOUNTING THE BLANK

For the pens in this chapter we used a split mandrel, also referred to as mandrel points. The split mandrel system consists of two short steel mandrels, which will hold each end of a barrel, and the appropriate bushings. The mandrel points are mounted in a drill chuck in the headstock and directly into the revolving tail center of the tailstock. The split mandrel is designed to allow for fast changing of the bushing and blank. It also requires less accurate alignment between the headstock and tailstock of the lathe than does the one-piece mandrel (see Fig 5.11).

The upper and lower blank sections should each be mounted separately on the split mandrel with the appropriate bushings as explained in the supplier instructions. The bushings provided by the supplier will determine the finished outside diameter of the barrels (see Fig 5.12).

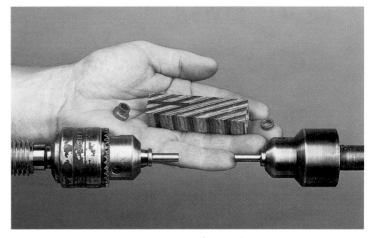

FIG 5.11 *The split mandrel, bushings and pen blank used for the lower section of the pen.*

FIG 5.12 *The split mandrel, bushings and pen blank used for the upper section of the pen.*

FIG 5.10 *Trimming with the barrel trimmer. The wooden adapter cannot be seen, but is inside the tube.*

FIG 5.13 *Rough turning the pen blank using a gouge. Notice that the ends have been turned smaller than the middle.*

FIG 5.14 *Making finishing cuts using the heel of a skew.*

FIG 5.15 *Using a narrow parting tool to cut the notch that will receive the metal trim ring.*

FIG 5.16 *Applying plastic polish as a finish.*

TOOL SELECTION AND USE

To turn the curve of a tapered pen, you should first turn down to the bushing on each end of the blank with a small gouge, leaving the blank thicker in the middle (see Fig 5.13). Next, carefully work the middle down, until a gentle curve remains. This curve is turned on both halves of the pen. Make the finishing cuts with a $\frac{1}{2}$in (13mm) skew (see Fig 5.14).

A small notch must be cut in the upper tube to accept a metal trim ring. After the pen has been turned and sanded, cut this notch $\frac{1}{16}$in (1–2mm) wide, completely through the wood to the brass tube, using a thin parting tool (see Fig 5.15).

SANDING AND FINISHING

For Dymondwood we recommend sanding to as fine as 600 grit, and even finer if a very high gloss is desired. Because of the plastic in Dymondwood, it can be buffed to a gloss without a top coat of finish. Adding a top coat will speed the finishing process to a certain extent, however, particularly if a very high gloss is desired. Stick wax works well, as does a fine plastic polish. The pens shown in this chapter received an application of a plastic polish. The polish should be applied with a soft cloth while the lathe is spinning (see Fig 5.16).

PRE-ASSEMBLY

Before beginning to assemble the pen, carefully read the instructions provided by the supplier. Assembly procedures vary depending on the supplier of the pen kit. Prior to assembly, the sharp corners on each end of the wood barrels should be sanded slightly (see Fig 5.17).

Some types of pen require a small notch to be cut in the finished barrel to receive the pen clip. If this step is necessary, start by selecting an area of the blank for the clip.

FIG 5.17 *Softening the sharp corners at the ends of the wood barrel.*

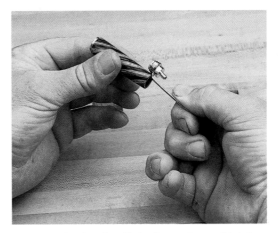

FIG 5.19 *Testing the clip in the notch, watching for correct depth and width.*

You may want to cover a small defect or highlight a part of the grain on the blank. A dremmel tool with a small grinding wheel can be used to grind this notch (see Fig 5.18). Grind the notch with the rotation of the grinding wheel cutting into the wood. This will stop the wood from chipping away from the brass tube.

Start by grinding a small notch in the desired area. Test the notch by turning the clip upside-down and placing it in the notch. This will allow you to check the

depth and width at the same time. Grind and test the notch until the clip fits snugly in place (see Fig 5.19).

Another method is to use a file. Some of the guesswork can be taken out of the process if the file used is the proper thickness for the required groove. The file can be clamped between the jaws of a vise or set inside a kerf cut in a piece of wood, so that only the necessary amount of the file is exposed. Drag the barrel across the edge of the file until the wood fixture prevents the

FIG 5.18 *Grinding the clip notch using a high-speed rotary tool with a small grinding stone.*

FIG 5.20 *Filing the clip notch using a simple fixture to control the depth.*

file from removing any more material (see Fig 5.20). This allows the filing process to go quickly while consistently making the correct size of notch to receive the pen clip.

FINAL ASSEMBLY

For the pens shown here we used a drill press (not switched on) and press jig for pressing the pen parts together. The drill press is used as a vise, while the press jig is used to keep the pen parts in line during assembly (see Fig 5.21). This method is very effective for assembling multiples of the same pen. It is well worth the time and effort that is needed to construct the press

jig. (A dimensioned drawing of the press jig is provided in Tips and Tricks, page 130.) Before beginning assembly, mount a $3/8$ x 2in (10 x 51mm) long bolt into the chuck of your drill press and place the press jig on the drill press table.

To assemble the rollerball, first lay the parts out according to the drawings provided by the supplier (see Fig 5.22). Place both barrels, with the large opening up, onto the stud of the press jig. The lower

FIG 5.21 *The drill press being used as an arbor press in conjunction with the press jig.*

FIG 5.22 *Part layout for the tapered rollerball.*

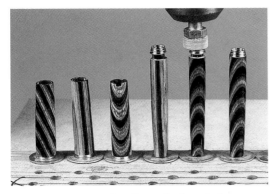

FIG 5.23 *Pressing the nib coupler into the lower pen.*

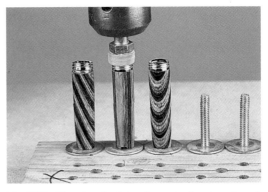

FIG 5.26 *Pressing the trim ring onto the upper barrel.*

FIG 5.24 *Pressing in the end cap.*

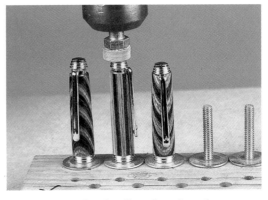

FIG 5.27 *Pressing the clip and cap into place.*

section is assembled by pressing the nib coupler into the large end of the lower barrel (see Fig 5.23). Next, flip the barrel over and press the end cap into the small end (see Fig 5.24). For the rollerball, press the spring (small end first) into the base of the refill and insert this into the barrel, then slide the nib over the refill and screw it into the coupler (see Fig 5.25).

To assemble the clip section, press the trim ring onto the notch end of the upper barrel (see Fig 5.26). Now flip the upper barrel over onto the stud and press the clip/cap assembly into the small end of the barrel. Make sure that the clip is aligned with the notch in the barrel (see Fig 5.27), then roll the nib spring up into a small roll and slide it into the large end of the top

FIG 5.25 *Screwing the nib over the refill and into the coupler.*

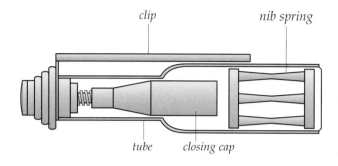

FIG 5.28 Cut-away showing the nib spring placement.

FIG 5.29 A modified Phillips screwdriver used to adjust the friction for holding the cap in place.

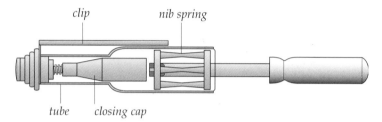

FIG 5.30 Cut-away of the upper barrel showing the cap adjuster tool.

FIG 5.31 The finished pens, with the tapered rollerball and fountain pens in the open and closed position.

barrel (see Fig 5.28). The nib spring provides needed protection for the nib as the pen is opened and closed.

The final step to complete the upper half of the pen is to insert the white closing cap. This is screwed in place, using a cap adjuster tool (a modified No. 1 Phillips screwdriver will also work), onto the threaded stud of the clip/cap assembly inside the upper barrel (see Fig 5.29). When you feel the closing cap bottom out, back it off with 1$\frac{1}{2}$ turns (see Fig 5.30).

To adjust the fit of the upper barrel to the lower barrel, place the writing nib into the cap assembly and test the fit. If the cap does not fit correctly, adjust the closing cap with the cap adjuster tool (or the No. 1 Phillips screwdriver) until it 'snaps' into place, with the cap fitting snugly against the coupler without creating a gap.

The only differences between the rollerball and the fountain pen are the writing nib and the refill. The nibs can be interchanged simply by screwing them in and out of the pen.

Generally the pen is assembled so that the grain match shows when the pen is in the closed position (see Fig 5.31).

CHAPTER 6

STYLE VARIATIONS ON BASIC PENS

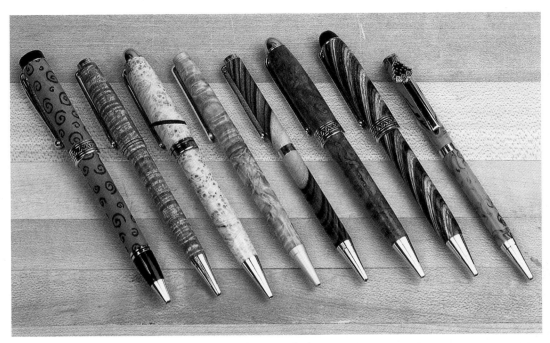

FIG 6.1   Several style variations can be added to basic pen designs.

LAMINATING

Laminating strips for contrasting color and grain can produce some exciting patterns and color combinations. Often small strips of wood are thrown away because they offer little value to a woodworker. A pen-maker can use these scraps to create some of the most interesting and unusual pen designs. Small strips of wood can be used in conjunction with a bland or contrasting piece of wood (see Fig 6.2). Strips of contrasting or matched exotic woods can be laminated to produce striking results. The combinations and designs are endless.

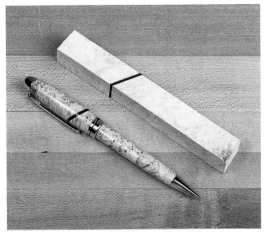

FIG 6.2   The simple addition of a contrasting strip of wood can add a touch of class to a more ordinary pen.

FIG 6.3 *Pen blanks and finished pens using laminated wood.*

CUTTING DIAGONALLY TO GRAIN

Diagonal cutting of parallel grain will produce an oblique pattern on the surface of the pen blank (see Fig 6.3). This method of cutting will enhance the grain pattern of woods that have strong parallel grain patterns, e.g. cocobolo, bocote, kingwood and Dymondwood, to name just a few.

There are a few things to be aware of when working with angled grain. First, since the grain is not in line with the tube it will tend to tear out during turning. This tearing can be reduced by being less aggressive while turning. Second, during drilling the drill bit tends to wander to the path of least resistance. Slower feed speeds while drilling and a good, sharp bullet bit will reduce this problem. Finally, use extra precautions to ensure a well-glued tube. If there are portions of the blank that are not glued to the tube, the short diagonal grain will have a greater tendency to tear away

from the tube. You may have some failures in the beginning, but the results of your success will make it worth the trouble.

LAYING OUT AND CUTTING

The oblique pattern created by cutting diagonally to the grain will be determined by the angle of the pen blank to the grain of the wood (see Fig 6.4). Start by drawing the profile of a blank diagonal to the grain on the surface of your wood. A felt-tip marker shows up well on most kinds of wood.

FIG 6.4 *Examples of the layout for one long pen blank and two half pen blanks.*

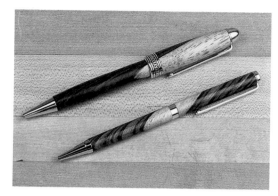

FIG 6.5 Finished pens showing the diagonal grain. The lower pen shows a book-match of sapwood at the center of the pen.

Smaller pieces of stock can be used to cut both halves of a pen blank side by side. In this case, the ends of the two halves are book-matched. This method works on woods that have contrasting grain patterns, such as cocobolo, olivewood, bocote and zebrawood (see Fig 6.5).

CLIP VARIATIONS

Pen clips come in all styles and shapes and are used for more than just clipping a pen to your pocket (see Fig 6.6). Many pen manufacturers have come to rely on the clip as a distinguishing feature of their pen designs. These exclusively styled clips may have trademarks on them and cannot be used by other manufacturers. Some clips will have company logos or are engraved for advertising purposes. Still other clips display themes such as sports, holidays or birthstones (see Fig 6.7). These 'theme' clips are used to promote the pen by adding another element of particular interest. Most pen suppliers offer a variety of such clips.

CARVING

Small, high-speed carvers can be used to make small carvings on pens (see Fig 6.8). Carved pens can be prepared and assembled in the same fashion as described in Chapter 3 (see pages 29–37). For carved

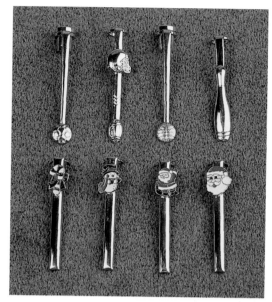

FIG 6.6 Assorted clip styles.

FIG 6.7 Completed pens with various 'theme' clips.

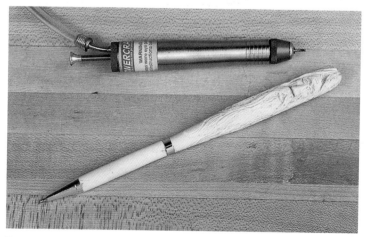

FIG 6.8 Small carver with mountain man pen by Brandon Wells.

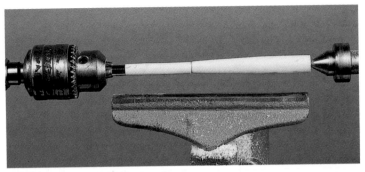

FIG 6.9 Chucking a pen blank using a bushing and a ¼ in (6mm) bolt or rod held in a drill chuck.

FIG 6.10 Carving a pen after turning and sanding.

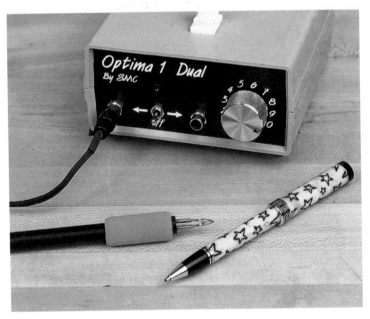

FIG 6.11 Hot-wire burner.

clip assembly to allow for the carved head. The upper half of the blank is not turned on a standard mandrel. It is turned by using a bushing and a ¼in (6mm) bolt or rod held in a drill chuck for the drive center. The other end is held with a revolving cup center (see Fig 6.9). As much of the pen as possible should be sanded and finished while it is on the lathe.

To hold the pen while carving, tape the finished portion of the blank onto a ¼in (6mm) bolt held in a vise, or carve it while it is still mounted on the lathe (see Fig 6.10).

WOOD-BURNING

Decorative wood-burning has been around for centuries. Pyrography comes from the Greek words *pur* (meaning 'fire') and *graphos* (meaning 'writing'). In the beginning a hot poker was used for burning. Today's hot-wire burners range from inexpensive one-pen machines to two-pen machines with many interchangeable points (see Fig 6.11). Pyrography on pens will allow you to express your wood-burning artistry.

The craft of wood-burning has traditionally been used on spoons, bowls, plates and in artistic pictures. The pen should first be prepared, turned and sanded using standard procedures. The pattern or picture to be burned on the pen can be sketched on freehand and then used as a guide. Another method that works well for transferring a pattern onto the pen is to make a photocopy of the desired image, wipe the surface of the pen with a generous coat of lacquer thinner, then press the photocopy against the surface of the pen. The lacquer thinner will lift the ink from the copy and provide a clear image on the pen (see Fig 6.12).

When selecting woods for pyrography, the best detail will be achieved when using light-colored woods that have a closed, even grain. Sycamores and maples work well.

pens, select woods that are easily carved, such as tupelo or basswood. Turn and shape the wood according to the carving that you have in mind. The mountain man pen shown here is made without the cap and

FIG 6.12 *Transferring a pattern to the surface of a pen.*

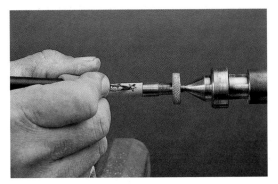

FIG 6.13 *Burning a simple pattern onto the surface of a pen using a hot-wire burner.*

Burning can be accomplished with the pen mounted on a mandrel and held in a vise, or while mounted on the lathe (see Fig 6.13). After the burning is complete, the pen can be lightly sanded to remove residual smoke, then finished as desired (see Fig 6.14).

FIG 6.14 *Completed pen-burned designs.*

WIRE-BURNING

A quick and easy way to add a touch of detail to a pen is to include one or more dark bands of accent by use of the wire-burn technique (see Fig 6.15). The process is simple. It does not require any cutting, drilling or gluing; and it requires the use of only one additional tool: a fine wire.

The width of the band created by wire-burning will vary depending on the gage of wire used (see Fig 6.16). For wire-burn on pens, most people prefer a very narrow line,

FIG 6.15 *Pens with wire-burn accents.*

FIG 6.16 *Varying widths of wire-burn created by different wires.*

FIG 6.17 *Simple wire-burn tools consisting of a guitar string and dowel handle.*

FIG 6.18 *Cutting a small v-groove to guide the wire while burning.*

requiring the use of fine-gage wire. A fine guitar string works well.

Holding the wire in your bare hands can be hazardous. This can easily be avoided by attaching each end of the wire to a handle made from a short section of dowel or other piece of wood (see Fig 6.17). To add handles to the wire, drill a $\frac{1}{16}$in (1–2mm) diameter hole through the side of the dowel, thread the wire through the hole and wrap it around the dowel two or three times. Put a drop of gap-filling CA adhesive in the drilled hole and on the exterior of a round toothpick. Drive the toothpick into the hole, wedging and gluing the wire in position, then trim off the excess toothpick with a knife or chisel.

After the pen is turned and sanded, use the toe of the skew to make one or more small v-grooves around the pen (see Fig 6.18). With the lathe rotating at a high rpm, pull the wire tight and, while keeping your hands free of the turning spindle, place the wire in the groove and apply moderate pressure (see Fig 6.19). The burn accent will generally appear rather quickly. In fact, since the wood around the brass tube may be only about $\frac{1}{32}$in (1mm) thick, do not get carried away and burn right through to the tube.

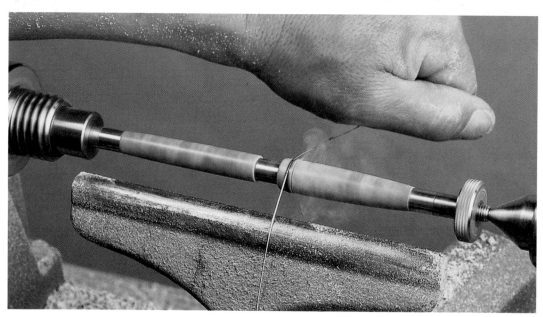

FIG 6.19 *Creating the wire-burn.*

FIG 6.20 *Applying steel wool to clean the surface of the wood near the burned area.*

After burning with the wire, clean the surface by gently sanding the area with fine abrasive or steel wool (see Fig 6.20). The pen is then ready for finishing coats and final assembly.

INLAYING

One way to add a nice touch to a wood pen is to include some crushed or powdered gemstone. The combination of stone and wood makes an excellent match since both are natural materials. Crushed and powdered stone offer a unique way to highlight the natural defects such as cracks, knots or wormholes. Several different gemstones can be bought in crushed or powdered form. Some of the more popular and colorful stones are turquoise (light blue), malachite (green), pink coral and chrysacola (blue) (see Fig 6.21).

The stone inlay pen is prepared and assembled in the same fashion as described in earlier chapters, except during the sanding process. Once the pen has been prepared and the blank turned to its final shape, stop the lathe and inspect the blank for defects. Larger defects are suitable for the crushed stone and smaller defects for the powdered stone. As you inspect the blank, you may want to enlarge the area so that it will accept more stone. A defect can be enlarged with a small rotary tool (see Fig 6.22).

Clean out the desired area and fill it with the crushed or powdered stone. Using

FIG 6.21 *Samples of crushed stone – green (malachite), pink (pink coral), blue (chrysacola) – used to highlight natural voids in the wood.*

FIG 6.22 *Enlarging small cracks to be filled with crushed gemstone.*

FIG 6.23 *Applying thin CA glue which penetrates and secures the powdered stone in place.*

water-thin CA glue, saturate the inlay. The CA glue will be drawn by capillary action down into the stone and surrounding wood and onto the tube (see Fig 6.23). For crushed stone this step should be followed by an application of thicker CA glue. The thicker glue will fill all the voids around the stone. As you fill the voids with stone and CA, try to use only enough materials to bring the defect even with the wood surface. Any excess stone and CA glue will have to be sanded by hand with the lathe stopped. To complete the process, sand and finish the pen with the lathe running.

BASIC TWIST PENS

Several style variations can be derived from the basic twist pen kit. Experimenting with possible variations can be a lot of fun and result in uniquely styled pens that are distinctly different from the standard twist pen design.

One variation that is very simple and yet attractive is to eliminate the metal center band. Without the center band, you have more freedom to explore other shapes toward the center of the pen, which can be thicker and more shapely. For example, a European style pen can be achieved simply by turning a gently curved taper on each half of the blank. The half toward the clip end of the pen should be slightly larger in diameter (see Fig 6.24).

FIG 6.25 *Notice the longer tube that is used for the writing tip end of the pen.*

FIG 6.26 *Standard twist pen bushings are used to size each end of the pen.*

An even nicer variation to the European style pen using a twist kit is to substitute one of the brass tubes used for twist pens with the longer brass tube of the European style pen kit. This tube is 2³⁄₈in (61mm) long rather than 2¹⁄₁₆in (52mm). Use the 2¹⁄₁₆in (52mm) long tube for the clip end of the pens, and then use the longer tube for the tip end (see Fig 6.25). This results in the separation between the two parts of the pen not being exactly in the center, making the pen more visually pleasing than the standard twist pen. The pen can be turned using the standard twist pen bushings. Since the center band is not included in the assembly, the only critical diameters are where the clip and the tip will be pressed into position (see Fig 6.26).

When assembling the pen, the transmission must be pressed in further to compensate for the longer tube length. This process is aided by using the 3¹¹⁄₃₂in (85mm) long v-block described in Chapter 3 (see page 37; see also Fig 6.27).

FIG 6.24 *These pens were made from the basic twist pen kit, but were turned with a European pen shape.*

Contrasting Bands

Another attractive touch that can be added to almost any pen is to include a band of contrasting wood or other material at the center or end(s) of the pen (see Fig 6.28). One might think that this can be achieved simply by adding a small piece of contrasting material to the end of a pen blank prior to drilling the hole for the brass tube. However, this does not give consistently good results, since the hole is not likely to be drilled perfectly perpendicular to the end of the blank. This causes the contrasting band to vary somewhat in width.

The procedure for achieving a perfectly aligned contrasting band takes a bit more

FIG 6.27 *The completed European style pen made from the standard twist pen kit.*

time, but the results are rewarding. First, prepare the pen blank following the standard procedure discussed in Chapter 3 (see pages 29–33). Mount the blank on a pen mandrel and turn slightly larger than the final diameter. Next, take a narrow parting tool and part through the wood at the end

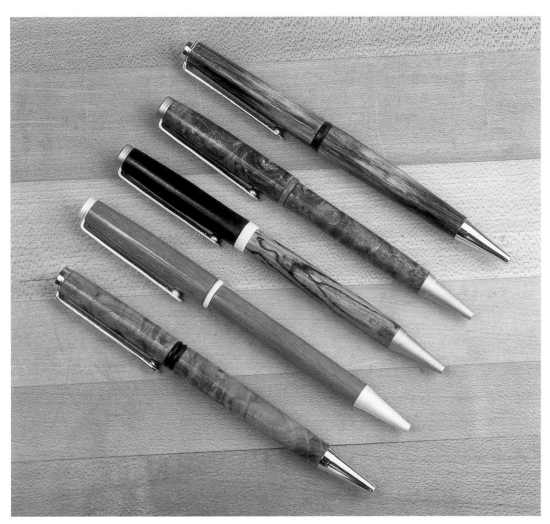

FIG 6.28 *Pens with contrasting bands.*

FIG 6.29 *This pen has been rough turned and cut with a parting tool to receive a contrasting band of wood.*

FIG 6.30 *Trimming the end of the blank.*

FIG 6.31 *The brass tube inside the blank after being barrel trimmed. (The tube is not glued in place.)*

FIG 6.32 *Cut off a short section of the blank to create the contrasting band.*

FIG 6.33 *Gluing the contrasting band section onto the end of the tube.*

of the blank until the brass tube is exposed (see Fig 6.29), then remove the pen blank from the mandrel.

To make the contrasting band, prepare a blank similar to one half of a pen blank by drilling a hole through the contrasting material to receive the pen tube. Without

using glue, insert a brass tube into the blank (to guide the barrel trimmer), then trim the end of the blank square using a barrel trimmer (see Figs 6.30 and 6.31).

Remove the brass tube from the blank and use a bandsaw to cut a short section off the end of the blank. This section should only be about 1/32in (1mm) longer than the desired length of the contrasting band (see Fig 6.32). Now place gap-filling CA glue on the outside of the exposed tube and on the inside of the band. Press the band, trimmed end first, over the end of the tube, and spray with CA accelerator (see Fig 6.33).

Once the glue has cured, use the barrel trimmer again to true up the rough end of the blank so that it is flush with the tube (see Fig 6.34). A pair of pliers and a bit of double-sided tape can be used to secure the blank while barrel trimming (see Fig 6.35).

Finally, remount the pen blank on the mandrel and complete the turning process (see Fig 6.36). Once this is complete, the pen can then be sanded, finished and assembled as described in Chapter 3 (see pages 34–37; see also Fig 6.37).

FIG 6.35 *Using pliers to secure the blank while barrel trimming.*

FIG 6.34 *Barrel trimming the second end of the contrasting band.*

FIG 6.36 *Completing the turning process by turning down the contrasting band.*

FIG 6.37 *The completed pen showing the contrasting band.*

TURNING A FLARE

Some people prefer the feel of a pen that is shaped with a flare or some other detail near the writing tip (see Fig 6.38).

A gentle flare can aid in gripping the pen, particularly during extended periods of writing. The flare shape is easy to turn with a small shallow gouge (see Fig 6.39). The diameter of the wood at the flare should be larger than the diameter at the bushing. However, the wood on the tip side of the flare should be at the same diameter as the bushing.

When turning the cove that creates the flare, take care not to reduce the diameter too far; the brass tube may be closer than you think (see Fig 6.40).

FIG 6.39   Cutting the flare with a small gouge.

FIG 6.40   Some people prefer the slightly different look and feel resulting from a gentle flare at the tip.

FIG 6.38   Pens with a flare turned near the tip.

CHAPTER 7

ALTERNATIVE METHODS OF PRODUCING PENS

FIG 7.1   Straight-barreled pens and pencils made using a router.

USING A ROUTER

Most woodturners make pens by turning freehand, using standard chisels and gouges. However, the design of many of the pens calls for a wooden barrel that is cylindrical in shape, having no tapers, curves or steps. Any of the pens that are designed to have straight barrels can also be made quickly and accurately without the wood ever being touched by a turning chisel. The process calls for the use of a router, guided by a router table that is built to set on the bed of a lathe (see Fig 7.2).

The sequence that follows details how to make a straight-barreled twist pen using a

FIG 7.2   Router table and lathe set-up.

router in conjunction with the lathe to do the actual 'turning'. Once the router jig is completed and the router properly adjusted, the process is not only efficient, but also consistently produces good results. The process of preparing the stock for routing is similar to that covered in previous chapters. Chapter 3 details the steps to follow up to the point of mounting the blanks on the lathe (see pages 29–33).

When making pens using a router, we recommend using the one-piece mandrel system secured in a morse taper and revolving tail center. The double mandrel is faster than the single mandrel, because both halves of the pen can be mounted and turned in one process.

The bushings provide a diameter gage to determine the finished outside diameter of the barrel. If the blanks are turned to the same diameter as the bushings, there will be a smooth transition from the wood to the metal parts of the pen. The router should be set to cut the barrel slightly larger than the diameter of the bushing. This will provide a bit of room for sanding.

The pen blank should be mounted on the double mandrel with at least one bushing at each end and one between the two halves of the pen blank. Do not forget to line up the grain match marks when mounting the pen blanks on the mandrel. The nut should hold all pieces on the mandrel firmly in place, but remember to avoid over-tightening the nut or the tailstock (see Fig 7.3).

The primary difference between turning the pens freehand and following the method shown here is the use of a router and a router jig. The jig guides the router and controls the depth of cut. The jig is fairly simple to construct. For dimensional stability, we recommend using either MDF or Baltic birch plywood. Figure 7.4 shows how the table is designed to be bolted onto

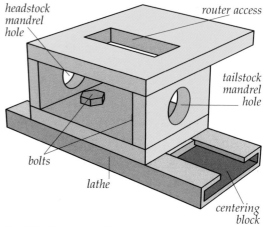

FIG 7.4 *The router jig.*

the lathe bed and allow the use of the headstock and tailstock for mounting the pen mandrel.

When making the initial set-up, check for accuracy by routing a spare pen blank. Before doing any sanding use a micrometer to measure the diameter along the routed cylinders. The diameter of the blanks should be consistent within about $5/1000$in. To fine-tune the adjustment of the router table on the lathe bed, use small shims between the base of the jig and the lathe bed. Strips of masking tape, strategically placed, will generally work for any shimming that may be needed.

After the jig is fastened to the lathe bed and properly adjusted, it is generally left secured in place throughout the entire turning, sanding and finishing process. Access to the mandrel is provided through the opening in the front of the router jig. The mandrel is inserted into place through the hole in the tailstock end of the jig. Finally the tailstock is moved into position and moderate pressure is applied to the end of the mandrel. Almost any lathe can be fitted with a router jig and used for the turning process.

We recommend a high lathe speed of between 3,000 and 3,500rpm. This helps to produce a better machined surface and increases efficiency during machining, sanding and finishing.

FIG 7.3 *Mandrel and pen blank.*

The tooling needed is both simple and readily available. Almost any standard router will work, but we recommend a router with a ¹/₂in (13mm) shank capacity rather than ¹/₄in (6mm). The larger shank reduces vibration and produces a cleaner cut. We have used several types of router bits with good results, including spiral-fluted straight bits, core-box bits, and dish-cutter bits. We have found that the dish-cutter produces excellent results and is the simplest to set up and adjust (see Fig 7.5).

The front opening to the table can be fitted with a sliding plexiglass shield for increased safety while not reducing visibility. Proper safety equipment is vital when using a router. A good face shield and hearing protectors are a must. However, if the router jig is equipped with a plexiglass shield, safety glasses may be sufficient rather than a full face shield.

When doing the actual routing, the following procedure is recommended. First, make sure the mandrel is secured between the headstock and tailstock. With the router and lathe turned off, place the router on the router jig toward the back of the opening so that the bit does not touch the pen blank. While holding the router in place with one hand, turn on the lathe with the other hand, then firmly grip the router with both hands and turn the router on.

It generally takes about three passes to machine the pen blank to the final diameter. The first pass is a roughing pass that should remove the square corners from the blank. The second pass should reduce the stock to within about ¹/₈in (3mm) of the final diameter. The third and last pass should then provide a smooth surface at the final diameter (see Fig 7.6). Each of the passes should be made with a slow horizontal feed

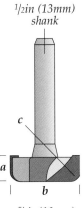

¹/₂in (13mm)
shank

a = ⁵/₈in (16mm)
b = 1¹/₄in (32mm)
c = ¹/₄in (6mm)
 radius

Fig 7.5 *The dish-cutter bit.*

Fig 7.6 *The first pass removes the square corners, an additional one or two takes the pen to its final diameter.*

rate to prevent chipping the wood. Each pass should also be made moving from left to right as you face the router. This direction of feed makes a 'climb cut' that produces a better surface than is achieved when feeding against the rotation of the router bit.

After the routing process is complete, turn off the router and lathe and allow both to come to a complete stop before lifting the router off the router jig and setting it aside. Inspect the blank for surface quality.

Sanding and finishing procedures are similar to those used when turning pens freehand. Although it may seem somewhat awkward initially, sanding and finishing will be more efficient if the router table remains secured to the bed of the lathe throughout the entire process.

After sanding and finishing is completed, the tailstock is released and backed away far enough to allow for the removal of the mandrel through the hole in the end of the router table (see Fig 7.7). The pen is then ready for assembly.

Fig 7.7 Applying finish with the pen still mounted inside the router jig.

USING A JEWELER'S LATHE

A small machinist lathe, sometimes called a jeweler's lathe, can be used to produce pens quickly and with consistent accuracy (see Fig 7.8). These small machinist lathes work on the same principles as larger machinist lathes. The cutter bits are locked in place by a cap screw on the tool post holder. The cutter is moved from right to left, in and out, by screw feeds.

Once the lathe is set up, this mechanical feed system allows the operator to turn the same pen easily time and time again. The machinist lathe is ideal for production work and requires very little skill to operate. They work best on straight-tubed pens, however. Tapered pens and other small projects that require more complex shapes are very difficult to produce with simple screw-feed lathes. Most of the small machinist lathes now offer an accessory woodturning tool base and tool rest for freehand turning.

The procedure for preparing the turning blanks is similar to that used when turning pens on a wood lathe. The procedure for mounting and making the pens, however, may vary slightly depending on the brand of lathe being used. For this chapter we used a Sherline lathe. This lathe requires a

Fig 7.8 The Sherline small machinist lathe.

FIG 7.9 *The two cap screws allow the position of the cutter to be easily adjusted.*

FIG 7.10 *During the first pass the square corners of the blank are removed.*

No. 1 morse taper, a one-piece mandrel, a revolving tail center and a special carbide cutter. The material shown here is 'Crushed Velvet'. The properties of Crushed Velvet are discussed in Chapter 8, Alternative Materials (see pages 100–101).

Once the revolving center has been secured into the tailstock, place the mandrel in the headstock. Slide a bushing onto the mandrel, followed by one half of the pen blank, then a second bushing, then the other section of pen blank, then another bushing, and finally the tightening nut. Bring the revolving center up into the dimple in the end of the mandrel. Be sure to check that the mandrel, pen blanks, tightening nut and revolving center are secured.

Position the cutter in the tool post holder by tightening the two cap screws (see Fig 7.9). With the lathe still turned off, rotate the cross-feed table back and forth to ensure that the cutter will travel from one end of the pen to the other. Set the travel stop so that it will prevent the cutter from hitting the mandrel or tightening nut. Set the lathe speed for about 3,500rpm.

MACHINING THE PEN

Rotate the blanks by hand to see if they clear the cutter and the lathe. Now turn the lathe on. Turn the cross-feed wheel until the cutter is in line with the corner of the first blank. Now, using the in-feed wheel, advance the cutter slowly into the blank

FIG 7.11 *Making the finishing pass.*

until you are removing about $1/8$in (3mm) off the corners of the blank. Once you have the correct depth set, slowly move the cross-feed table down the pen, thus completing the first pass (see Fig 7.10).

Once the pass has been completed, turn the in-feed wheel by about $1/8$in (3mm) and make a second pass. After a couple of passes, stop the lathe and inspect the surface that has just been cut. If the surface is cut clean you may consider taking deeper cuts or making a faster pass. If the surface is rough and chipped, take a lighter cut and use a slower feed speed to improve the surface being cut. When the pen blank is about $1/16$in (1–2mm) larger than the diameter of the bushings, make a light finishing pass (see Fig 7.11). Be careful not to advance the cutter into the bushings.

Once the blank has been cut to size, rotate the cutter out of the way and use standard techniques for sanding and finishing (see Figs 7.12 and 7.13). You will notice that the quality of the cut will vary, depending on the type and density of the material being worked. By decreasing the depth of cut and reducing the feed rate you will be able to improve the quality of cut. As a general rule, the harder and denser the wood, the cleaner the cut.

Most of the rosewood family will produce an excellent finishing cut. Woods like elm and maple burl will often tear to a certain extent. Softer woods which produce torn grain can be stabilized with thin superglue, as discussed in Tips and Tricks (see page 126).

FIG 7.12   Plastic polish being applied to provide the finishing luster.

USING AN ORNAMENTAL MILL

If you want to add a new twist to your pens, try using an ornamental mill. Barley twists, rope twists, straight flutes and reeds, and spiral flutes and reeds are just a few of the decorations you can create with ornamental milling (see Fig 7.14). The variety of designs is essentially limited only by your imagination.

Ornamental milling machines have been around for many years. However, most quality ornamental milling systems are quite expensive and not practical for use by hobbyists or even medium-production woodworking shops. Ornamental milling machines are also typically designed for relatively large work like furniture parts, or architectural components such as newel posts and columns.

The recent proliferation of turned wooden pens and other small, turned projects, however, has encouraged at least one manufacturer of ornamental milling machines to design a model specifically for the hobbyist and small shop (see Fig 7.15).

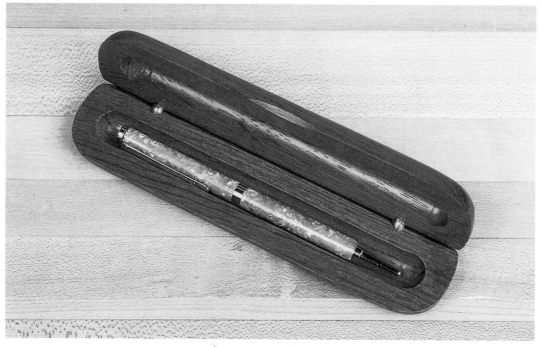

FIG 7.13   The finished pen made from 'Crushed Velvet'.

FIG 7.14 *Pens made using an ornamental milling.*

Another relatively inexpensive ornamental milling machine that could be used for making pens is the Router Crafter, by Sears.

The pens in this section were produced using the Legacy 500, an ornamental mill recently introduced by Phantom Engineering, and specifically designed for making decorative designs on a variety of small, turned items such as pens, key chains and letter openers. The mill is designed to be compatible with standard pen mandrels and other turning accessories. It comes equipped with a standard No. 2 Morse taper with 1in (25mm) x 8 threads at the headstock, and a dead center in the tailstock. With ornamental milling a dead center is often sufficient, because the lathe rotates at such a slow rpm while the router removes the material.

While the system will handle stock up to 5³/₄in (146mm) in diameter and 36in (914mm) long, it is also ideal for working with smaller items such as pens. The Legacy 500 incorporates standard ornamental milling capabilities such as an indexing system for uniformly spaced detailing, a

spiral drive system for controlling the travel and rotation of the work piece, a pattern follower allowing shaped contours such as on the European style pen, and X-Y-Z milling capabilities for control in all three axes. The machine is surprisingly versatile.

Creating the variety of designs possible through ornamental milling is an extensive topic that could easily be the subject of a complete book. Here we will introduce the concept of ornamental milling by showing how to produce a straight-barreled pen with a spiral twist, and a European style pen with spiral or straight fluting.

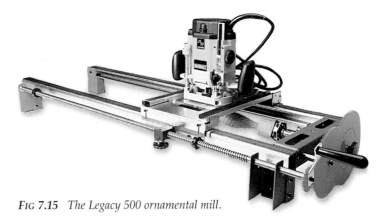

FIG 7.15 *The Legacy 500 ornamental mill.*

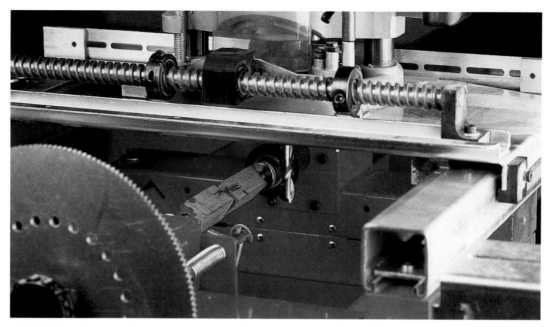

FIG 7.16 *The router bit is positioned to machine on the side of the pen blank.*

STRAIGHT-BARRELED PEN WITH OCTAGONAL TWIST

Imagine a pen that is octagonal in cross-section rather than round. Now imagine taking the octagonal pen and twisting it from each end like a piece of licorice or decorative iron. What you would have then we call an eight-sided twist, or an octagonal twist. The procedure below details the steps involved in milling an octagonal twist pen using an ornamental milling machine.

The process for preparing the pen blanks is identical to that discussed in Chapter 3 (see pages 29–34). For the twist pen we will use a double mandrel with a No. 2 Morse taper. The pen blank is mounted on the pen mandrel in the same way as when turning them on a lathe. The ornamental milling machine is capable of milling pens with almost any number of sides desired. We have found the most pleasing number of sides to range from six to twelve. Here we will show how to make an eight-sided twist.

If you were to cut the blank in half anywhere along the length and look at the end, what you would see would be a perfect octagonal cross-section. To mill this shape

you need to use a $^1/_2$in (13mm) diameter, two-flute, straight router bit and mill from the side of the stock (see Fig 7.16). This is different from most milling operations, which are performed by positioning the bit directly above the stock and plunging straight down onto the material. The pitch can be adjusted to make a gradual twist or a tight twist. We have found a 6in (152mm) pitch with eight sides to be very attractive and easy to produce.

With the machine set for a 6in (152mm) pitch and the bit positioned on the back side of the pen blank, the stop is set on the Y-axis drive screw to control the diameter of the pen. The closer the bit is to the center, the smaller the diameter it will cut. If the bit is positioned so that it is just touching the bushings, the finished diameter of the pen will be the same as the bushing. We prefer to make the diameter slightly larger by setting the stop so that the bit is between $^1/_{64}$ and $^1/_{32}$in (0.5–1mm) from the bushing. Then the stops are set on the X-axis drive screw for the proper length of the pen (see Fig 7.17). Take care that the bit will not hit the mandrel or the nut securing the blanks.

FIG 7.17 *Setting the stops on the X-axis.*

FIG 7.19 *Sliding the split nut along the X-axis.*

FIG 7.18 *Milling the first pass.*

Starting at the tailstock end so that the router bit will be climb-cutting, turn the router on and slowly bring it up to the Y-axis stop, then mill toward the headstock end (see Fig 7.18). Once it has reached the stop at the headstock end, simply reverse the direction of feed and mill back to the tailstock with the bit in the same position. This pass will be undercutting and should produce a clean finish cut. When the router comes to the stop, turn the Y-axis drive screw to move the router back away from the stock. This completes the first pass.

For the second pass it is necessary to rotate the blank by 45° or 1/8th of a turn. This can easily be performed by repositioning the router along the X-axis lead screw. Note where the router carrier is on the X-axis ruler, and then open the split nut and slide the carrier 3/4in (19mm) toward the headstock and close the split nut (see Fig 7.19).

A little math is needed to explain why we move the carrier 3/4in (19mm). To calculate how far to move the carrier tray for multiple-pass spirals, simply take the

FIG 7.20 *Milling another pass.*

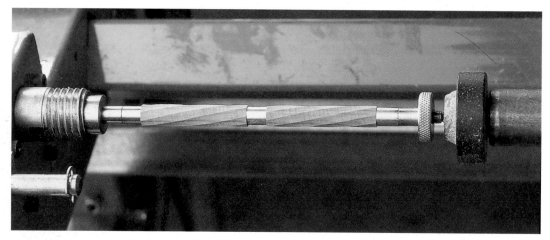

FIG 7.21 *Milling is complete and the pen is ready for sanding.*

pitch divided by the number of passes. In this case the pitch was set for 6in (152mm) and we will make eight passes, therefore, we take 6 (or 152) divided by 8 to get the ³⁄₄in (or 19mm) spacing for each pass.

Once the carrier has been repositioned by ³⁄₄in (19mm), drive the carrier back to the starting position and bring the router up against the stop in the Y-axis to mill the second pass. Again you will mill to the headstock end and back. Simply reposition the carrier by ³⁄₄in (19mm) by opening the split nut as for the second pass to make the third pass (see Fig 7.20). Repeat this process of milling and repositioning until you have milled all eight passes (see Fig 7.21).

Once the pen blank has been milled, the easiest way to sand it is by using flutter sheets mounted in a drill press. The flutter sheets create a sanding brush that will mold around the surface of the pen. We have found that 320 grit abrasive works well. It will not take off too much from the edges, but makes the surfaces satisfactorily smooth. Grits coarser than 320 are too aggressive and will quickly sand away the crisp edges and fine detail created by the milling process. When sanding with the flutter sheets, be sure to soften the corner at each end of each barrel (see Fig 7.22).

With the blank milled and sanded, it can be finished using a variety of methods. One quick and simple method is to apply French polish with a rag, then buff the finish by hand using a dry rag. The sheen can be cut back by using 0000 steel wool, or increased by additional buffing with a fine paste wax. The pen is then ready to be assembled following the procedure given in Chapter 3 (see pages 35–37; see also Fig 7.23).

OCTAGONAL, EUROPEAN STYLE PEN

Two primary steps are required to complete the octagonal European style pen (see Fig 7.24). The first step is to mill the profile of the pen. The second step is to mill the shoulder for the center band. For the first step, the Legacy Ornamental Mill can be used as a copy lathe. A stylus follows a template that can be used repeatedly. The major difference between a lathe and a mill is that the lathe rotates the stock at high speeds while a slow-moving tool is used to remove the material. A mill uses a cutter

FIG 7.23 The completed spiral twist pen.

FIG 7.24 Octagonal, European style pens.

rotating at a high speed to remove material while the stock is rotated slowly.

Phase 1: Milling the profile

To mill a curved profile you will need to make a template for the stylus to follow. We have found ¾in (19mm) MDF to be an excellent material for templates. It is easy to cut and, most importantly, the edges can easily be sanded perfectly smooth. Keep in mind that any rough areas on the template will be transferred to the surface of the pen. Once the template is ready it needs to be

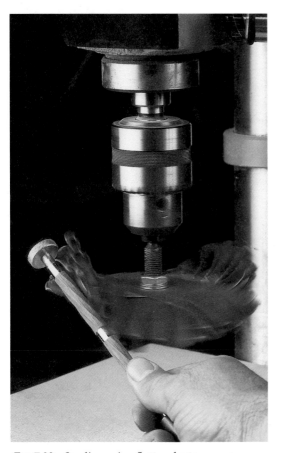

FIG 7.22 Sanding using flutter sheets.

FIG 7.25 *The shape of the pen is controlled by the stylus riding along against the template.*

FIG 7.26 *The pen blank mounted and ready for milling.*

positioned so that the center of the stylus is at the starting point of the template. Make sure that the template is parallel to the machine and secure it to the table using screws or double-sided tape (see Fig 7.25).

To mill the pen, start by mounting the pen blank on the mandrel (see Fig 7.26), then position the router so that a 1/2in (13mm) spiral router bit is centered at the headstock end of the blank. Now loosen the stylus and position the router so that it touches the bushing on the pen mandrel. Then back it off a few thousandths of an inch, set the stylus against the template and lock it in place.

Now that the template is positioned correctly and the stylus is set in place, you can begin to mill the pen blank by locking the stock in place with the index pin and slowly moving the router carrier from the tailstock to the headstock end (see Fig 7.27). If the pen blank is relatively large in diameter, you may want to make a couple of passes, removing a little stock each time.

After the first surface of the blank has been milled, release the indexing pin and rotate the index plate by three holes, or 45° (see Fig 7.28). Now repeat the same process to mill the second surface (see Fig 7.29). This process is repeated on all eight surfaces of the blank to complete the octagonal profile of the pen (see Fig 7.30).

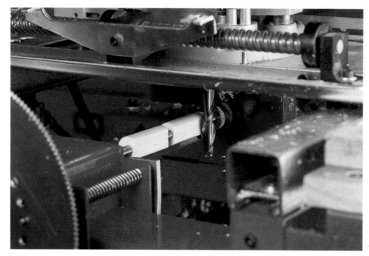

FIG 7.27 *Milling the first pass.*

FIG 7.28 *Setting the index plate.*

FIG 7.29 *Making the second cut.*

FIG 7.30 *The pen after milling each of the eight sides.*

Phase 2: Milling the shoulder to receive the center band

The same router bit is used to cut the shoulder for the center band. However, the cut is made on the bottom of the bit rather than from the side. Begin by marking the pen blank where the shoulder will end, then slide the router bit into place over the top of the blank and set the stops for the X-axis. Next, set the plunge depth and mill the shoulder by bringing the bit slowly over the center as you rotate the stock (see Fig 7.31). The pen and mandrel can now be removed from the mill and sanded, using flutter sheets as previously shown, to finish the pen (see Fig 7.32).

FIG 7.31 *Milling the shoulder for the center band.*

FIG 7.32 *The completed octagonal European style pen.*

CHAPTER 8

ALTERNATIVE MATERIALS FOR MAKING PENS

FIG 8.1 Some popular alternative materials for making pens.

POSSIBLE ALTERNATIVES

Turned pens can be made from a wide variety of materials. Essentially, any material that is solid, stable, and can be worked with standard woodworking tools, is a potential candidate for pen material. This creates intriguing and almost unlimited opportunities for the craftsman who is willing to use some imagination, creativity and, occasionally, a bit of humor. In addition to pens made from fine exotic woods, we have seen pens made from a variety of partially decayed woods; man-made wood products such as laminated construction beams, plywood, particle board, Dymondwood and dyed Colorwood; an array of cast synthetic materials, including Corian, Crushed Velvet and Decora; other natural materials such as antler, horn, bone, leather and stone; and even resin-saturated cow manure.

This chapter covers several types of materials that can be used in pen-making. Each of the materials has characteristics which respond somewhat differently to cutting, drilling, gluing, turning, sanding and finishing. These differences will be discussed throughout the chapter.

ANTLER

Antler is a beautiful and extraordinary material (see Fig 8.2). One of the most interesting facts regarding antlers is that the animals produce a new set each year. The old set of antlers is simply cast off and discarded. As a result, the supply of antler is renewable, requiring neither the killing of the animal nor the removal of an appendage that cannot grow back, as is the case with tusks and horn. Furthermore, antler is a surprisingly resilient material. While it is quite hard, it is not excessively brittle. It is apparent that nature designed antler to take considerable abuse.

It is interesting to note that the replacement of a full set of antlers each year requires a growth rate that is nothing short of phenomenal and classifies antler as the most rapidly growing bony structure in the animal kingdom. During the peak growing period, elk antler will increase in length by nearly 5in (127mm) per week. The antlers of a large Alaskan moose may grow by nearly

FIG 8.2 Elk and deer antler.

a pound (370g) a day, reaching over 65 pounds (24kg) before the process is complete. During this time the animal must consume food containing many pounds of calcium and phosphate.

Because of the size, most craftsmen are primarily interested in the portion of the antler at the base, where the antler meets the skull. This section, often referred to as a 'crown', 'rosette', or 'burr', is relatively large and dense. It is commonly used for belt buckles, bolo ties, and as a medium for scrimshaw work. For pens, however, the upper branches of antler are more appropriate because they are smaller in diameter, essentially round in cross-section, more widely available and much less costly to purchase (see Fig 8.3).

FIG 8.3 Elk burrs and branches.

FIG 8.4 *Section cuts of elk and deer antler. Elk antler, shown on the left, tends to be more colorful than deer antler, shown on the right.*

Antler from deer and elk is most commonly used for making pens. The color of antler is generally white to gray and varies somewhat with each piece. Elk antler is more colorful than deer antler. In the porous inner sections of elk antler, the white background is interrupted by irregular dots ranging in color from dark burgundies to grays and blacks (see Fig 8.4).

Antler responds well to turning using either shearing, scraping or shear-scraping techniques. The resulting shavings are similar to that of wood – shearing produces curls and scraping produces powder. Antler does have a grain direction similar to wood, although it does not have growth rings. Generally, no special tools are required for working antler. It is, however, much harder than wood and also more abrasive on tools. As a result, the cutting edge of tools must be restored more regularly when turning antler than when turning most woods.

One characteristic of antler that poses a challenge for lathe work is the porosity of the inner portion. When drilling, the antler must be held firmly in place and the rate of feed reduced somewhat to prevent the drill bit from following the path of least resistance and wandering into the softer porous sections. When gluing the tube into the pen blank, a generous application of glue to line both the inside of the antler and

the outside of the tube will help to reduce the porosity of the antler immediately surrounding the brass tube (see Fig 8.5).

During the turning process, the porous inner core must be reinforced with CA glue. To do this, first turn the antler to very near the final shape and diameter of the completed pen – $\frac{1}{32}$in (1mm) oversize is about right – then flood the surface of the antler with thin CA adhesive. Rotate the lathe slowly by hand to prevent the CA from flowing to the bottom and dripping off. While the thin CA glue is still wet, flood the surface again with gap-filling CA adhesive (see Fig 8.6). By capillary action, the thin CA adhesive will help pull the thicker gap-filling CA into the pores. The glue can then be set using CA accelerator. The process may need to be repeated.

The entire surface of the antler should be covered with CA glue and the glue set. Next, the surface glue is removed by simply turning away the excess. If the process is successful, there will be no voids where the antler was previously porous. The pen can then be sanded using standard techniques. Antler takes a nice polish without the aid of

FIG 8.5 *Elk antler mounted on the lathe, ready to begin the turning process.*

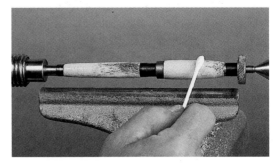

FIG 8.6 *Using CA glue to reinforce the porous inner portion of the antler.*

FIG 8.7 The completed European style pen made from elk antler.

finish, so little or no finish is necessary. In fact, CA adhesive itself provides a rather good finish. If an additional finish is used, it should not contain oils, as this may turn the antler a yellow color. French polish works well as a finish, as does plastic polish and also Renaissance paste wax (see Fig 8.7).

Other than the patience required to work the dense outer portion of antler and to reinforce the porous inner section, standard drilling and turning procedures can be used. Extra precaution should be taken to avoid breathing dust from antler.

Spalted and Punky Woods

Apparently it is not known where the term 'spalted' wood originated, or when it was that the beauty of spalted wood first caught the eye of the woodworker (see Fig 8.8). Spalted wood is wood that has been infected by a variety of fungi which, during the natural process of decay, have created a mosaic pattern of light and dark areas often bordered by black and brown lines. These lines, called 'zone lines', may be as broad as 3/16in (5mm), or so thin that they are barely visible. Irregular multiple-color patches, bordered by dark zone lines, provide

FIG 8.8 Spalted wood pen blanks.

striking visual contrast. The result is some of the most spectacular wood available to the woodworker.

Although it is safe to assume that spalted wood has been around for as long as trees have, it was not until the late 1970s that spalted wood became accepted as a medium for woodworking.

Since the late 1970s the popularity of spalted wood has increased dramatically among woodworkers, and particularly among turners. It is no surprise, therefore, that spalted wood has been adopted by pen-makers. Quality spalted wood makes some of the finest pen material available.

However, the nature of the wood presents its own challenges to the craftsman.

The process of spalting produces results which are both exciting and disappointing to the woodworker. While the decay process is causing wood to take on interesting changes in color and pattern, this same process is often breaking down the cellular structure of the wood. It is not unusual for a piece of wood that contains spalting to also contain sections consisting of a number of different degrees of density, ranging from sound, undecayed wood, to wood so soft and 'punky' that it can be easily destroyed

FIG 8.9 *The awl stuck into this pen blank illustrates the softness of this piece of spalted English beech.*

FIG 8.10 *Stabilizing the soft spalted wood with thin and gap-filling CA glue.*

with a scrape of the fingernail. This inconsistency of density in spalted wood can create significant difficulties when trying to machine, sand and finish the wood. Often the wood may have sections that are so soft they simply cannot be worked cleanly using traditional methods (see Fig 8.9).

Not all spalted woods, however, have decayed to the point that the cellular structure is destroyed. There is often a magic moment in the process of decay when the fungi have produced spalt patterns but not yet advanced to the point of destroying the wood. The decay process can be halted at that point simply by drying the wood. If you are fortunate enough to obtain such spalted wood, it may be worked using similar processes as with almost any sound wood. If, however, the decay process has advanced to the point where the structure of the wood has been destroyed, the wood may not be workable unless it is stabilized.

Many pen suppliers stock a variety of pen blanks of spalted or other softer woods, such as redwood burl, that have been commercially stabilized through impregnation with a plastic resin. Working with commercially produced stabilized wood is discussed in the next section. It is possible, though, to stabilize pen blanks during the turning process.

This can be accomplished in a similar manner as discussed earlier for working with antler. Apply a liberal amount of CA adhesive when gluing the brass tube into the wood blank. When turning, the pen should first be turned to near its final size. It should then be flooded with a combination of thin and gap-filling CA adhesive, and the adhesive should be hardened using CA accelerator (see Fig 8.10). The excess glue can then be turned away with a gouge or skew. At this point, inspect the surface to ensure that there are no soft areas remaining. It may be necessary to apply additional CA adhesive to a few spots.

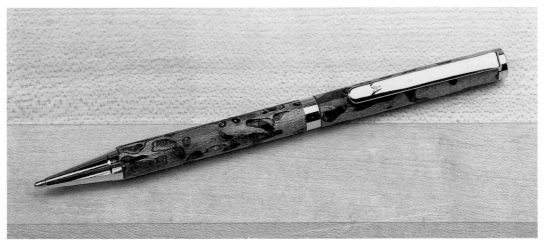

FIG 8.11 *CA glue was used to harden this piece of spalted, decayed English beech. Though quite interesting in appearance, this wood is not practical for use unless it is stabilized with CA or other resin.*

FIG 8.12 *A sampling of stabilized wood pen blanks.*

Sanding and finishing can be accomplished using standard techniques.

The technique of hardening soft wood using CA adhesive is quite handy and can be used whenever a portion of a pen blank is particularly soft and difficult to work with (see Fig 8.11).

STABILIZED WOOD

As already discussed, spalted and decayed wood may be very spectacular in appearance but can be difficult to work with due to soft, punky sections. Wood containing soft sections can be impregnated under high pressure with a plastic resin.

The result is a wood/plastic composite that is relatively hard and consistent in density throughout (see Fig 8.12).

The popularity of spalted wood for pens has encouraged commercial enterprises to produce stabilized wood pen blanks for the market. Some of the most popular stabilized woods used in pen-making include soft burl woods such as box elder burl and redwood burl, as well as spalted woods including maple, hackberry, English beech, sycamore, pecan and others. These blanks are typically distributed by retail suppliers of pen mechanisms. The availability of stabilized wood has provided small-scale woodworkers with the opportunity to work with materials not previously practical. Stabilized woods, however, have different working properties from most common woods.

Since stabilized wood is a composite material of wood and plastic, it has inherent working properties of both plastic and wood. Stabilized wood is harder, denser and somewhat more brittle than untreated woods. It is also more sensitive to heat and excess heat can quickly cause a pen blank to split while being drilled. Slower feed speeds are therefore required when drilling and cutting stabilized woods. Once on the lathe, stabilized wood works much like a very dense hardwood. It generally turns and sands well. The plastic in the wood can often be buffed to a good, high polish without the use of a finish. If additional finishing is desired, almost any good wood finish will work well. Plastic polish is also an effective option.

DYMONDWOOD

Dymondwood is a unique and innovative manufactured wood material made better by science and technology (see Fig 8.13). It is made from natural 1/16in (1.5mm) hardwood veneers (usually birch or maple) that have been impregnated with specially formulated phenolic resins and permanently colored with dyes. These veneers are then bonded under high temperature and tremendous pressure. The result is Dymondwood, a uniform multi-layer wood product with a wide range of unique physical and mechanical properties not available in conventional woods.

Dymondwood's beauty, richness, texture and grain cannot be matched by any other natural material. It is very stable and resistant to changes in humidity or moisture. Since Dymondwood is

FIG 8.13 A few samples of Dymondwood.

impregnated throughout with resin, there is no need for additional finishes. It may simply be buffed to a satin or gloss finish. Dymondwood is one of the best pen materials available to pen-makers today.

Although Dymondwood is very dense, it can be machined with standard woodworking tools and machinery. The manufacturer does recommend using carbide cutters whenever possible, however. When drilling, high-speed steel twist drills and brad point bits can be used, but these bits will overheat easily and dull quite quickly. We have found that the 'bullet' drill bits cut better and drill straighter (see Fig 8.14).

Dymondwood can be used with the grain oriented parallel to the pen tube to make straight-grained pens, or it may be cut on a bias to produce blanks with a diagonal grain pattern. The diagonal pattern is particularly striking. Although it takes more time to prepare a Dymondwood pen blank with diagonal grain, the results are well worth it.

When cutting angled blanks with Dymondwood, unless you are careful, the process will result in excessive waste of a rather expensive material. One good way to virtually eliminate unnecessary waste is to start with a piece of Dymondwood that is cut to the thickness, and at least $1/2$in (13mm) longer than the desired pen blank. Draw a line diagonally from corner to corner on the surface of the material. This angle will determine the pattern of the finished surface (see Fig 8.15).

Cut the Dymondwood on the diagonal line. Lightly sand each of the outside edges (not the cut edge) of the block before gluing the sanded edges together with gap-filling CA or epoxy adhesive. To ensure a good

FIG 8.15 *The layout of Dymondwood blanks for a diagonal grain pattern.*

FIG 8.16 *Place glue on both surfaces.*

bond, press the surfaces together with a generous amount of glue, and set aside on a piece of waxed paper (see Fig 8.16). Allow the glue to cure, then sand or scrape any excess glue off the blank. Set your bandsaw for the required width of the pen blank and cut the blank into strips. Square the ends of the blanks with the bandsaw.

For gluing the tubes into the blanks, we recommend the use of polyurethane glue that will expand during the drying process to fill voids and gaps that would otherwise be left by CA adhesives. Although we are not certain, our hunch is that polyurethane

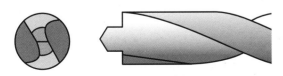

FIG 8.14 *The tip of a bullet bit.*

glue may reduce heat-checking in completed pens, which is sometimes a concern with Dymondwood.

Although you may have to sharpen them more often, standard high-speed steel turning tools work perfectly well for turning Dymondwood. Set the lathe for about 3,000–3,500rpm and take light cuts to reduce chipping and tear-out.

Dymondwood can be sanded with regular sandpaper up to about 600 grit. If a very high gloss finish is desired, you will need to sand to 1200 grit or higher. Since Dymondwood contains plastic throughout, it can be buffed on the lathe to a fairly high gloss without the use of any finish. However, most people prefer to add a top coat of finish. A Hut wax stick that contains fine abrasive compounds is a popular finish for Dymondwood. A plastic polish can also be used to increase gloss and paste wax will produce a high or low sheen (see Fig 8.17).

COLORWOOD

Colorwood is a plywood composed of various color combinations of maple veneers, approximately $1/16$in (1–2mm) thick (see Fig 8.18). The veneers are dyed in a vacuum, then bonded under tremendous pressure. Unlike regular plywood, where the grain of each layer of veneer is alternated at 90° angles, the veneers in Colorwood all run in the same direction. This makes the material work in a way which is more similar to solid wood than plywood. Various grain pattern effects can be achieved when Colorwood is cut at an angle. Colorwood is not impregnated with resin, therefore it can be worked easily with regular wood-working tools (see Fig 8.19). It tends to contain brighter colors than Dymondwood. As described in the section on Dymondwood, striking oblique patterns can also be created with Colorwood.

FIG 8.17 Dymondwood cut on an angle can result in striking grain patterns on the finished pens.

FIG 8.18   *Samples of Colorwood pen stock.*

Colorwood can be machined with standard woodworking equipment. It is slightly more abrasive on tools than most hardwoods, but will be friendlier to your equipment than Dymondwood. High-speed steel tools are recommended.

Brad point drill bits work well with Colorwood. We have found that the bullet drill bits cut better and drill straighter, and this will be of particular help if you decide to turn the blank on an angle. When turning Colorwood pen blanks cut on an angle, however, you will need to be more cautious. Make sure that you take light cuts to reduce chipping and tear-out.

Cyanoacrylate, epoxy and polyurethane adhesives all work well on Colorwood for gluing the tube in place.

Colorwood sands much like natural hardwoods. Sand with abrasive paper and proceed to at least 400 grit. As with most hardwoods, we recommend the use of French polish or Mylands Friction Polish when finishing pens that are made of Colorwood (see Fig 8.20).

FIG 8.19   *Ripping a Colorwood pen blank on the bandsaw.*

FIG 8.20   *Completed Colorwood pens.*

ALTERNATIVE IVORY, HORN AND TORTOISESHELL

In past centuries, ivory was a common material used by turners for making small but fine items such as buttons, musical instrument parts and various types of knobs. Ivory, however, is no longer available. Fortunately, in recent years a material referred to as 'alternative ivory' has been developed and made available to woodturners and other craftspeople. Similar substitutes for horn and tortoiseshell have also been introduced (see Fig 8.21).

The composition of each of these materials is quite similar, as are their working properties. Alternative tortoiseshell, however, is translucent and even somewhat transparent, particularly when thin in section. As a result, alternative tortoiseshell does not lend itself well as a material for pens, since the brass tubes often show through. Ivory and horn substitute do not present this problem since they are opaque.

These substitutes are a cast polyester material. Woodturning suppliers that carry alternative ivory generally stock it in the form of solid rods, varying in diameter from 1/2in (13mm) to 3in (76mm). While the material is relatively expensive (except when compared with the real thing), it can be used efficiently, resulting in very little waste. It is quite brittle, however, and will fracture easily if aggressive cuts are made using traditional turning tools and methods. With a light touch and a little practice, progress can be quick and satisfying.

Generally speaking, the following suggestions apply. Easy does it. Aggressive cuts of any kind often result in serious tear-out. Aggressive cutting with skews and gouges, as we commonly do when working wood, will cause the material to fracture without warning. Gouges can be used, but scrapers with the burr honed off produce the best results (see Fig 8.22). The angle of grind should be quite blunt, approximately 75°. The lathe speed should also be reduced

FIG 8.21 From left to right: cast rods of alternative tortoiseshell, ivory and horn.

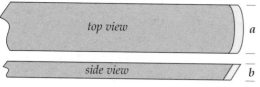

top view a

side view b

$a = \frac{1}{2}in\,(13mm)$ $b = \frac{1}{4}in\,(6mm)$

FIG 8.22 A slightly domed scraper.

FIG 8.23 An inevitable nuisance associated with turning many synthetic materials is the clinging shavings that build up on the work.

significantly to less than 1,000rpm, even when working small diameters.

The shavings produced are very light yet stringy and tend to cling to the work, which can become a bit annoying (see Fig 8.23). Fortunately, the shavings can quickly be removed with a soft bristle brush or a wire brush (see Fig 8.24). Alternative ivory can be sanded and buffed much like a good, dense hardwood. No finish is needed, although a fine wax or plastic polish will add to the sheen if desired.

When drilling, the feed rate should be reduced to prevent shattering. If the drill rpm is too high, it can cause the material to become hot enough to melt. With a little practice you will learn the limitations of the

FIG 8.24 Removing the clinging shavings.

material and be able to adjust accordingly. The results are pleasant both to the eye and to the touch (see Fig 8.25).

FIG 8.25 From left to right: finished pens made from alternative ivory, tortoiseshell and horn. The pen in the center is alternative tortoiseshell: notice that the brass tube can be seen in the lower section of the pen.

CRUSHED VELVET AND SIMILAR SYNTHETICS

Crushed Velvet is a cast synthetic (see Fig 8.26). Its working properties are quite different from wood and working with it takes a bit of getting used to. It can be machined with standard woodworking equipment. We recommend using a bandsaw when ripping and crosscutting.

Because of the low melting point of Crushed Velvet, extra care must be taken to prevent overheating. When drilling, set the drill speed at around 600rpm. Brad point bits can be used with good success, but once again we have found that the bullet drill bits cut cooler and drill straighter.

CA, epoxy and polyurethane adhesives all work well.

Standard high-speed turning tools also work satisfactorily when turning Crushed Velvet. Keep in mind that Crushed Velvet has a low melting point. When using a bevel rubbing cut, do not push the bevel too hard against the blank, as the plastic may soften

and begin to melt. Use a small scraper for finishing cuts (see Fig 8.27).

Crushed Velvet can be sanded with regular sandpaper up to about 1200 grit. Use a light touch when sanding in order not to melt the blank or load the paper full of

FIG 8.27   Producing a finishing cut, using a small scraper, on Crushed Velvet.

FIG 8.28   Sanding using wet/dry abrasive and water.

FIG 8.26   Crushed Velvet and other cellulose acetate pen blanks.

FIG 8.29 *A fine luster can be given to Crushed Velvet using a buffing wheel.*

SOLID SURFACE MATERIALS

Solid surface material is a non-porous, synthetic material widely used for countertops and other similar applications (see Fig 8.31). It is a blend of natural minerals, pigments and acrylic resins which can be machined with regular woodworking equipment. It can be sanded and buffed to a matt or gloss finish. Solid surface materials can be drilled as well as turned using standard high-speed tools. Many solid surface materials are designed to look like natural stone. The natural look and ease of

sanding particles. For best results use wet/dry sandpaper and water. Keep a small container of water on hand for dipping the sandpaper. The water will act as a coolant and will wash the sanded particles away from the sandpaper (see Fig 8.28). Wet/dry sanding is well worth the effort in order to produce a quality finish.

To finish Crushed Velvet, gently buff with a soft wheel and fine grit compound to produce a gloss finish (see Fig 8.29). Another method of finishing is to use a liquid plastic polish. These polishes are made of liquid waxes mixed with fine abrasive compounds to produce a glossy finish (see Fig 8.30).

FIG 8.31 *Solid surface pen blanks.*

FIG 8.30 *Completed pens made from Crushed Velvet and other cellulose acetates.*

FIG 8.32 Polishing a Corian pen using liquid plastic polish to produce a fine gloss.

working make such materials a good choice for pen-making.

Solid surface materials are made by many companies, including Dupont (USA), Wilsonart (USA), Corian (UK) and others. Each manufacturer uses a slightly different formula to produce their desired colors and appearance. It is difficult to tell them apart simply by looking at them, however, you will notice some differences in how they each respond to drilling and turning. Pen suppliers usually offer a good selection of solid surface materials that can be used for pen blanks. The standard stock is generally manufactured in sheets of two thicknesses: $\frac{1}{2}$in (13mm) in a wide selection of colors, and $\frac{3}{4}$in (19mm) in fewer selected colors. Pen suppliers then cut the pen blanks from the sheet material.

As with the other synthetics, brad points can be used with good success, but we have found that the bullet drill bits remain cooler. For working with these materials the drill speed should be slowed to around 600rpm.

Although manufacturers of solid surface material recommend a special adhesive, we have found that CA and epoxy work well when gluing solid surface materials to the brass tube. These adhesives can also be used to glue two pieces of solid surface material together when pieces thicker than $\frac{1}{2}$in (13mm) are required.

Solid surface synthetics respond well to turning using high-speed turning tools and standard techniques. They can be sanded with regular sandpaper up to about 1200 grit. For best results use wet/dry sandpaper

FIG 8.33 Finished pens made from solid surface countertop materials.

and water. Keep a small jar of water next to the lathe in order to wet the sandpaper. The water will act as a coolant and will wash the sanded particles away from the sandpaper. Sanding with water is rather messy, but it speeds up the process, reduces the amount of powdery dust that may be inhaled and produces good results.

When finishing, gently buff with a soft wheel and fine grit compound to produce a gloss finish. Plastic polish can also be used to produce a fine gloss (see Figs 8.32 and 8.33).

POLYMER CLAY

While the use of polymer clay for making pens is at present largely unexplored, it seems that this remarkable material offers unending possibilities (see Fig 8.34). Polymer clay is a relatively new material, having been around since the mid-1960s. During the past decade this material has been discovered and accepted as a versatile medium for a variety of art and craft work. It lends itself particularly well to illustration figures, wearable art and jewelry.

Although the term 'polymer clay' is quite descriptive of the material, it is not actually a clay. It is a polymer, a thermo-set plastic which, when baked at a moderate temperature in a conventional oven, becomes fused and hardened. Polymer clay is a compound consisting primarily of polyvinyl chloride (PVC) with the addition of a plasticizer to increase flexibility, a filler to add body and texture, and pigments to give color.

Polymer clay is now readily available in local stores that supply art and craft materials. It comes in small bricks that are moldable, much like other clays (see Fig 8.35). Prior to being baked, it can be formed, sculpted, rolled, extruded, sliced and stamped. In its hardened state it can be cut, drilled, carved, machined, sanded and

FIG 8.35 Bricks and canes of polymer clay.

FIG 8.34 A variety of pens made from polymer clay.

finished. It can be manipulated to imitate metal, wood, fabric, stone and other materials. Although polymer clay becomes hardened when baked, it does not become rock hard. It is, however, durable enough to be used in making pens.

There are several excellent, comprehensive books about polymer clay detailing its properties, how to work it, what tools are needed, and a vast variety of methods that can be used to create different effects. For our purposes here, we will only touch on a few basics that will provide some ideas and simple methods of using polymer clay in making pens. Here are four methods of using polymer clay in pen making.

METHOD 1

The first procedure is the simplest and does not even include the use of the lathe. This method consists of wrapping the exterior of the pen tubes with polymer clay, and forming the clay to achieve the finished size and shape of the pen barrels. The tubes are then baked to harden the clay, and the ends are trimmed clean with a barrel trimmer. The pen is then assembled and ready to use.

Although this procedure is quite straightforward, the variations that can be achieved in design, color combination, pattern and even surface texture are literally unending. The materials and tools needed are simple and inexpensive (see Fig 8.36). The pen shown in the following sequence is made using only two materials: black polymer clay and gold foil. The tools consist of an 8in (203mm) square ceramic tile, an acrylic rod used as a rolling pin, a sharp craft knife, and an autopsy blade or wallpaper blade.

First, a small ball of polymer clay is gently kneaded in order to improve its consistency and warm it to body temperature. The clay is then rolled into a thin sheet (see Fig 8.37). A pasta machine can also be used to produce a thin sheet of clay that is perfectly consistent in thickness. The final thickness of the sheet is determined by the difference between the diameter of the brass tube and the diameter of the bushing appropriate for the pen.

For this straight-twist pen, the final thickness of the clay will be about $1/32$in (1mm). However, since gold leaf is to be added to the surface of this pen, the clay should initially be rolled slightly thicker. After the layer of gold leaf is added, the clay is rolled to the final thickness to create a cracked appearance on the surface of the pen (see Fig 8.38).

The sheet can then be trimmed with a sharp, straight-edged blade, in this case an autopsy blade, to match the width of the tube. You can also use a straightedge and a standard craft knife. One end of the sheet should also be squared off with the blade (see Fig 8.39).

The polymer clay sheet is then placed gold side down and rolled onto the brass tube. Where the two ends meet, the sheet is cut with the blade to form a clean match (see Fig 8.40). Where the ends join, it is necessary to press the clay together to form a good bond (see Fig 8.41). The wrapped tube is then rolled gently on the tile to give the pen a consistently smooth surface (see Fig 8.42).

The pen barrels are now ready to be baked and hardened. While being baked,

FIG 8.36 A few basic tools and materials used in working with polymer clay.

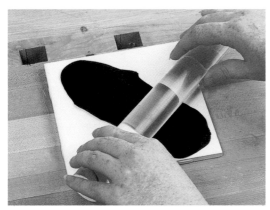

FIG 8.37 *Rolling the warmed ball of polymer clay into a thin sheet.*

FIG 8.38 *The clay stretches as it is rolled, but the gold leaf separates, creating a cracked effect.*

FIG 8.39 *Trimming the clay sheet to the approximate size with a sharp, straight-edged blade.*

FIG 8.40 *Rolling the clay onto the brass tube and matching the ends.*

FIG 8.41 *The ends of the polymer clay sheet are blended together.*

FIG 8.42 *Rolling the clay on the tile produces a smooth final surface.*

the polymer clay on the surface of the tube should not be in contact with any other surface. This can be accomplished by placing a small dowel through the brass tubes and laying the ends of the dowel on the edges of a cake pan, suspending the barrels while they bake (see Fig 8.43). The

pen barrels should be baked in a preheated oven at 270°F (140°C, Gas Mark 1) for between 60 and 90 minutes, depending on the thickness. For the very thinly wrapped tubes, 60 minutes is adequate. Tubes that are wrapped thicker for subsequent turning should be baked for 90 minutes.

METHOD 2

The second procedure using polymer clay is a variation of the first. This method, however, does include the use of a lathe. As with the first procedure, the pen tubes are wrapped with clay, but they are wrapped over-size, slightly larger than the desired final diameter (see Fig 8.44). After the barrels are baked, they can then be cleaned and trimmed with a barrel trimmer. The barrel trimmer can be mounted in a drill or set into a handle and operated by hand (see Fig 8.45).

FIG 8.45 *Trimming the end of a hardened clay barrel with a barrel trimmer.*

FIG 8.46 *Turning the polymer clay pen.*

FIG 8.43 *These pen tubes have been wrapped with polymer clay and are ready to be baked in an oven.*

FIG 8.47 *Sand with water and wet/dry abrasive.*

Next the tubes are mounted on a pen mandrel and turned, much like working with other synthetics such as Crushed Velvet or Decora (see Fig 8.46). You will find that the polymer clay is relatively soft and easy to turn using standard shearing techniques. Care should be taken not to ride too heavily on the bevel of the tool as this may mar the polymer clay. Polymer clay is quite heat sensitive, so be careful to avoid creating excess heat while sanding. We recommend sanding with wet/dry abrasive and water (see Fig 8.47). After sanding, the surface can be buffed with a clean cloth. A fine paste wax, such as Renaissance wax, may be applied to add gloss.

FIG 8.44 *These pen tubes have been wrapped with a heavy layer of polymer clay and then baked to harden the clay.*

METHOD 3

The third procedure, fundamentally different from the first two, may be the easiest method for the woodturner who has never worked with polymer clay. This method is essentially the same as that used for working other pen materials. Polymer clay can be purchased in pre-made canes available in a variety of colors and patterns (see Fig 8.48). These canes are solid, most commonly round in cross section, and are generally about 2in (51mm) long. Two canes will yield one pen.

When purchased, the canes will not be baked and this should be done prior to drilling or turning. Baking instructions are provided by the clay manufacturer and included with the clay. These may vary slightly, depending on the composition of the clay. Follow the supplier's instructions precisely. If no instructions are provided, bake the canes in a preheated oven at 270°F (140°C, Gas Mark 1) for 90 minutes.

Once the canes are hardened, the pen-making process is similar to that discussed in Chapter 3 (see pages 29–37). The working properties of the clay, however, require some minor adjustments and extra caution. When drilling the cane to receive the brass tube, slow the rpm down to less than 1,000, and proceed gently. Polymer clay is quite sensitive to heat. Too much friction or heat at any point during the process can cause the clay to soften or fracture. If the clay crumbles, it is an indication that the clay was under-baked.

METHOD 4

The fourth method is a slight variation on the previous technique. This option is to make your own solid canes rather than buy pre-made ones. This opens an unlimited range of possibilities in colors and patterns. Once the canes are formed and baked, the process is the same as given above. The process for making your own canes is, however, beyond the scope of this book. Included in the list of books on page 159 are references to excellent sources for detailed instruction on making canes from polymer clay (see Fig 8.49).

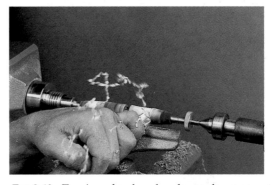

FIG 8.49 Turning a hand-made polymer clay cane.

FIG 8.48 Purchased polymer clay canes.

FIG 8.50 The finished pen, made from a simple, hand-made polymer clay cane.

CHAPTER 9

TIPS AND TRICKS

FIG 9.1 Pen blanks stacked and ready for drying.

DRYING GREEN BLANKS

The woods you acquire for making pens will often be 'green', or at least not fully dried. Unless you are certain that your pen wood is dry, you should assume that it is not, and you should dry the wood yourself prior to drilling the holes to receive the brass tubes. The drying process is simple enough, but is very important and should not be overlooked. Pen stock dries quite quickly if it is first cut to a rough thickness and width of between $1/16$ and $1/8$in (2–3mm) over the desired final blank dimensions. The blanks should be left long and not cut to length until after they are dry. This will reduce waste, as there may be some defects which appear during drying. Rip the blanks to rough size using either a bandsaw or table saw, and with a bold marker write the current date on a few of the blanks.

To dry the blanks, stack them log-cabin style with plenty of room for air circulation (see Fig 9.1). After a few days, take several of the blanks and weigh them using a gram scale. Record the date and the weight. Restack the blanks and let them dry for another few days, then weigh the same blanks and again record the weight. Continue drying and occasionally weighing the same blanks. Once the blanks stop losing weight, you will know they are dry in relation to the relative humidity in your area. The stock is now ready to be cut to length and drilled as needed for the desired pen.

The drying process can be accelerated by stacking the blanks and heating them in a microwave. Be patient, however, because the finer exotic woods are often very sensitive to heat. Begin microwaving on low heat settings for less than 30 seconds and allow to air-cool thoroughly. Repeat the process, each time slightly increasing the cooking time by a few seconds. The blanks should only feel warm to the touch and never get so hot that they cannot be held comfortably. Once you think the blanks are dry, allow them to acclimatize for two or three days and then check the weight. Keep in mind that you may have forced too much water from the wood and the blanks may actually need to gain moisture from the air in order to be stable and ready to work. Repeat the air-drying and weighing cycle until the weight of the blanks remains constant from day to day.

Pen blanks can also be dried in a shop-made drier such as the one pictured in Fig 9.2. This drier, designed for drying thin slices of fruit, is excellent for drying pen blanks. The box was constructed with a gentle heating element in the bottom, a fan to force air movement, and screen trays that allow even circulation of heat. The blanks should be arranged so that they do not

FIG 9.2   Pen blanks drying in a fruit drier.

touch each other and air is allowed to circulate freely around each blank. The end grain of woods that are particularly heat sensitive should be coated with wax or glue to reduce the possibility of end-checking during the initial stages of drying.

CUTTING BLANKS

Cutting the blanks to width and length can be done using a variety of saws. However, the bandsaw is the machine of choice because of its thin cutting kerf and because it allows the operator the ability to cut short and thin pieces of wood safely. By making some simple jigs for the bandsaw you will be able to produce pen blanks quickly, accurately and with a high degree of safety.

SLIDING TABLES

The sliding cutoff table, with an adjustable stop bolt, is a simple jig that can be used effectively for cutting pen blanks to length on the bandsaw (see Figs 9.3 and 9.4).

FIG 9.3 *This sliding table is easy to make and allows the pen blanks to be cut to length safely, accurately and with very little waste. (The blade guard is raised so the details of the fence and the stop screw may be seen.)*

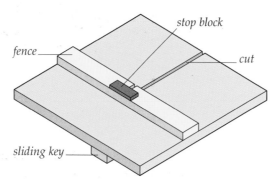

FIG 9.4 *The sliding table.*

To make the sliding cutoff table, start with a piece of $3/4$ x 12 x 12in (19 x 305 x 305mm) sheet material such as medium density fiberboard (MDF) to make the cutting table. Cut a strip of hardwood for a sliding key to fit into the miter groove of the bandsaw table. The fit should be snug enough not to allow any movement from side to side in the groove, but loose enough to allow the key to slide freely back and forth along the groove. Center the cutoff table on the bandsaw table and mark the position of the blade and the slot for the miter gage. Using a square, draw a line from the miter gage marks and attach the

hardwood key in between the marks with glue and small nails or screws.

Once the glue has dried, place the miter strip and cutoff table onto the bandsaw and make a cut about 7in (178mm) long into the table. Remove the table from the saw and draw a pencil line indicating the position of the fence at a right angle to the cut. Cut a $5/8$ x $2^1/2$ x 12in (16 x 64 x 305mm) long strip of hardwood for the fence. Align the fence to the pencil marks, then glue and screw the fence board to the sliding table.

To make the adjustable bolt stop, cut a $5/8$ x $1^1/4$ x 8in (16 x 32 x 203mm) long piece of hardwood and drill a $1/4$in (6mm) diameter hole into the end. This hole will receive the adjustment bolt and should be about $2^1/2$in (64mm) deep. Screw a $1/4$ x 2in (6 x 51mm) long carriage bolt into the drilled hole. Glue the stop block to the miter fence, with the end of the bolt being about $4^1/2$in (114mm) away from the bandsaw kerf. The stop block and adjustable bolt allows you to cut and adjust the length fast and accurately. The screw is simply turned in or out in order to match the length of the pen blanks you are cutting (see Fig 9.5).

One additional feature that is good to have on your sliding cutoff table is a stop to prevent the likelihood of you (or anyone else) inadvertently cutting through your sliding table. This feature is easy to add to your jig. Simply glue a small block of wood

FIG 9.5 *A sliding table in use on the bandsaw.*

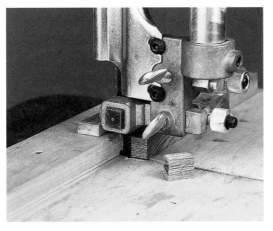

FIG 9.6 *The sliding table showing the stop in place. Notice that the saw teeth cut slightly into the fence before the guide blocks contact the stop and prevent the blade from cutting too far.*

about $^3/_8$ x $^1/_2$ x 1in (10 x 13 x 25mm) to the top of the fence and in line with the path of the blade. The stop should be back from the front edge of the fence about $^1/_4$in (6mm). This will vary depending on the design of your bandsaw guard; the aim is to allow the teeth of the blade to penetrate into the fence up to about $^1/_8$in (3mm) and for the sliding table to be stopped when the blade guard contacts the stop block (see Fig 9.6).

REMOVABLE STOPS

Once the sliding cutoff table has been built, it can be operated using a variety of simple modifications. To cut pen blanks to their full length (approximately $4^1/_2$in (114mm) depending on the style of pen) adjust the screw to extend the appropriate distance from the blade and use it as a stop. (This is the cut that is shown in Fig 9.6.) When separating the pen blanks into the two halves of a pen, a simple removable stop block, such as that shown in Fig 9.5, can be placed against the screw to give the proper length.

For pens that require two wood sections of different lengths, such as the European style pen, two different removable stop blocks can be used. These can be moved in and out of place against the stop screw as needed (see Fig 9.7).

MARKER LINES

Another variation on the sliding table is simply to draw bold pen marks on the fence indicating the proper length from the blade that pen sections should be cut. Figure 9.8 shows the cutting of a short-length section for a European style pen. Notice the two bold lines drawn on the fence that indicate where to position the end of the stock in order to cut the proper length. This method is simple, quick, and produces good results.

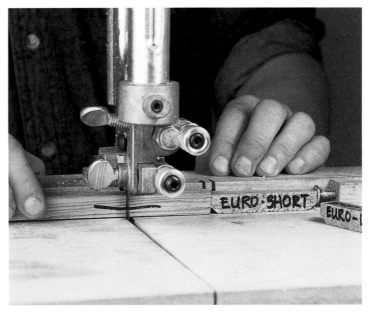

FIG 9.7 *Cutting the short section of a European style pen by using a removable stop block to determine the correct length.*

FIG 9.8 *Cutting one section of a pen blank to length using the sliding table marked with a pen to indicate the appropriate length.*

SECURING STOCK

GATE JIG MOUNTED ON A BASE

One of the best methods to secure the blank while drilling is to use a shop-made 'gate jig' which includes a base that functions as an auxiliary table (see Fig 9.9). The jig consists of a permanent base made from $3/4$in (19mm) thick sheet material, a $1/4$in

FIG 9.9 *The gate jig provides a safe, quick and positive method of securing stock during drilling.*

(6mm) thick replaceable subfloor that is temporarily nailed to the permanent base, a $3/4$in (19mm) thick fence of solid hardwood that is glued into a groove in the base, a swinging gate of solid hardwood that is hinged to the fence, and a hinge (see Fig 9.10).

The blank being drilled sits on end on the $1/4$in (6mm) thick subfloor. To help reduce blowout, the subfloor should be replaced occasionally to assure good support for the blank being drilled. Directly underneath where the pen blank is positioned, a large hole – about 1in (25mm) in diameter – is drilled through the $3/4$in (19mm) base of the jig. This hole allows shavings to escape down through the base of the jig. If the jig is positioned directly over the hole often found in the metal drill press table, shavings will not build up even when drilling several blanks successively. Another simple feature that reduces the build-up of shavings near the hinge is to cut away a section of the sub-base, allowing shavings to escape underneath the gate at the hinge end of the jig.

The swinging gate is about $1/2$in (13mm) longer on the left end than the fence. This makes it easier to open the gate after the blank is drilled. Also note that the hinge is on the right end of the jig. This is so the left hand can open and close the jig while the right hand is used to operate the drill press. (Left-handed turners will probably want the

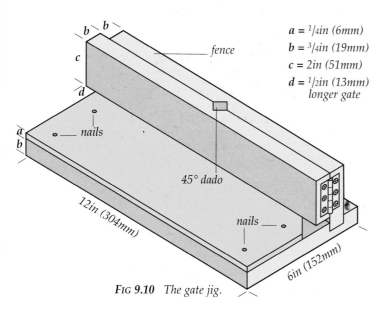

$a = 1/4$in (6mm)
$b = 3/4$in (19mm)
$c = 2$in (51mm)
$d = 1/2$in (13mm)
   longer gate

fence

45° dado

nails

nails

12in (304mm)

6in (152mm)

FIG 9.10 *The gate jig.*

FIG 9.11 *Drilling a pen blank using the gate jig.*

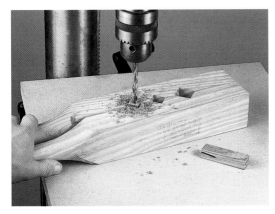

FIG 9.12A A hinged jig by Hut products.

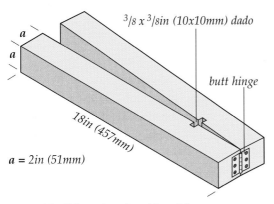

³/8 x ³/8in (10x10mm) dado

a

a

butt hinge

18in (457mm)

a = 2in (51mm)

FIG 9.12B Dimensions for a hinged jig.

hinge to be on the left end of the jig.) The dados down the fence and gate should be aligned with each other and be slightly narrower than the thickness of the thinnest pen blanks you plan to drill. The dados may be cut at either 45° or 90° to the face of the fence and gate.

You will find that this jig is safe and easy to use, provides excellent control and allows for quick clamping and removal of the blanks (see Fig 9.11). It can be used with pen blanks of varying thickness, including round blanks such as rods of alternative ivory. With the base of the jig clamped in a bench vise, it provides an equally good method for securing blanks for trimming with a barrel trimmer.

DRILL PRESS TABLE

Although the gate jig can be held in place by hand while drilling, an ideal method of centering and securing the pen blank for

drilling is to use the gate jig in conjunction with a drill press table that has X and Y axis adjustment capabilities, as shown in Fig 9.9. The jig can be secured in place on the drill press table using double-sided tape. Centering the blank on the bit is a matter of adjusting the position of the table by threading it forward or backward and left or right. This method is particularly handy when drilling several blanks of similar dimensions, but it also allows for easy adjustment when drilling blanks that are of varying dimensions.

SIMPLE, HINGED JIG

A variation of the gate jig is the simple, hinged jig. This jig operates on the same basis as the gate jig but does not have a fixed fence that is fastened to a base (see Fig 9.12A). The hinged jig has the advantage of being simpler to construct than the gate jig (see Fig 9.12B), yet, if properly made and used, it will hold a pen blank straight and secure during the drilling process. Hinged jigs are also available commercially.

MODIFIED QUICK-GRIP CLAMP

Another simple method of holding pens while drilling is to use a modified Quick-Grip clamp. Cut a v-groove or square dado in a set of wooden jaws and secure the jaws to a Quick-Grip clamp with double-sided tape (see Fig 9.13).

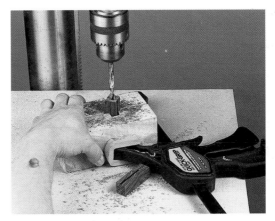

FIG 9.13 Drilling using a Quick-Grip clamp modified with a set of wooden jaws.

MODIFIED PARALLEL JAW CLAMP

Auxiliary jaws can also be secured to the jaws of a parallel jaw clamp with double-sided tape (see Fig 9.14). They eliminate the need to disassemble and cut grooves into the jaws of the clamp. Ease of opening and closing the clamp is improved by hinging together the jaws at its handle end. A leather hinge, fastened in place by staples or screws, and glue, works well. It allows the parallel jaw clamp to be opened and closed easily by adjusting one handle only.

DRILLING

Drilling can be one of the most tricky (and temperamental) processes in pen-making. Problems that often occur include the blank blowing out, the drill bit overheating, the drill bit wandering, and off-center drilling. The design of the drill bit being used is often an important factor. For advice on drill bit selection, see Chapter 2, pages 15–17.

FIG 9.15 These pen blanks have been destroyed by blowout during drilling.

BLANK BLOWOUT

Blank blowout is caused by the drilling pressure breaking through the last $^1/4$in (6mm) of unsupported wood at the bottom of the blank (see Fig 9.15). This problem is more prominent with very dense woods like ebony, pink ivory and Dymondwood. These woods can be quite brittle and have very little give. Following are a few suggestions to help reduce this problem.

- Use a bullet-type bit: this generally reduces problems with blowout.
- Make sure to slow down the rate of feed as the drill bit passes through the bottom end of the blank.
- Cut pen blanks about $^1/8$in (3mm) thicker than required. This will help strengthen the blank during drilling.
- For woods that are particularly difficult to drill without causing blowout, cut the blanks about $^3/8$in (10mm) longer than the required tube length, then set the depth stop on the drill press to drill the hole $^1/8$in (3mm) deeper than the length of the tube. This will leave $^1/4$in (6mm) of solid wood in the bottom of the blank that can be trimmed off later using a bandsaw. This extra support at the base of the tube should eliminate most problems with blank blowout during drilling.

FIG 9.14 Using a modified parallel jaw clamp to secure a pen blank for the drilling process.

OVERHEATING

Overheating during drilling of the blank may cause hairline cracks to develop in the wood. Many of these may not be noticeable at the time of drilling, but will appear after the pen has been turned and finished (see Fig 9.16). This situation is most prevalent in dense exotics and in Dymondwood. The following tips should offer some help with this problem.

- Use a bullet-type bit to help reduce overheating.
- Clear the chips from the bit regularly by using short strokes and also by occasionally backing the bit completely out of the blank.
- Keep the bit sharp. This is important because sharp bits will produce much less heat.
- Clean the flutes of the drill often, especially when drilling oily woods such as cocobolo. To clean the flutes, gently press a small scrap of wood or a small brass brush against the drill as the drill is spinning (see Fig 9.17).
- Keep the drill bit cool. Allow the bit to cool between drilling each blank, or cool it more with water. Cooling can be accomplished by padding the bit with a damp cloth or sponge while the drill press is stopped (see Fig 9.18).
- Some of the softer synthetic materials such as Crushed Velvet and celluloid acetate will melt if drilled at high speeds. For better results, slow the drill speed down and ease up on the drilling pressure. Slowing the drill press rpm may also help reduce overheating in exotic woods that are very dense and heat sensitive.

OFF-CENTER DRILLING

Properly centering the drill bit on the wood that is being drilled can prevent problems that may occur not only during drilling, but later on as well.

A precisely centered drilled hole will reduce the probability of the bit drilling too close to the side of the blank. If the hole is centered on the blank, turning time is reduced somewhat because the blank can be roughed down more quickly.

Possibly the most important reason for having the hole centered on the blank is that it results in a better grain match once the pen is assembled.

FIG 9.16 When drilling pen blanks, the drill bit can easily become overheated.

FIG 9.17 Using a brush with short brass bristles is one way to keep the drill bit clean during drilling.

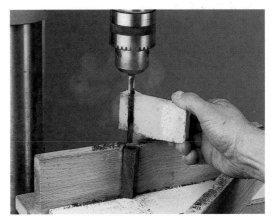

FIG 9.18 Cool the drill bit with a damp sponge while the drill press is stopped.

Since the hole drilled in a pen blank is relatively deep, often the drill bit will follow the grain and wander off center, occasionally even drilling through the side of the blank (see Fig 9.19). The following tips help to reduce the probability of the drill bit wandering.

- Keep the drill bit sharp. Dull or improperly sharpened cutting edges will often lead the drill bit off the desired path. This will almost always happen if the bit is sharpened so the leading point is not at the center of the bit.
- The bullet-type bit is the best we have found for drilling straight holes in a variety of materials.
- Reduce the feed speed while drilling.

GLUING IN THE BRASS TUBE

Gluing the brass tube into the pen blank is a relatively simple process. However, depending on the type and quality of the pen blank being used, some precautions or additional steps may be necessary.

Throughout the chapters of this book we have shown a variety of methods for applying adhesive inside the hole in a pen blank. We also discussed the properties of different adhesives in Chapter 2 and have shown the application of various adhesives throughout the book. Here are a few additional tips that may be helpful.

CLEANING THE TUBE

Brass tubes often become coated with a film of oxidation which may interfere with the adhesion process and prevent a good bond between the tube and the blank. If the tubes look dark or discolored, they should be cleaned before being glued inside the blank. The oxidation can quickly be removed by sanding the outside of the tube with 100 grit abrasive. This rough and cleaned surface will allow glue to bond better to the tube (see Fig 9.20).

STRENGTHENING INSIDE THE BLANK

Strengthening from inside the blank can often save your pen blanks. Some materials, such as pink ivory, ebony, burl woods,

FIG 9.19 These blanks show the undesired result of a drill bit wandering off-center during the drilling process.

antler, spalted woods and Dymondwood may have hidden defects, punky areas, or even hairline cracks caused by overheating during drilling. Strengthening the wood from the inside with thin CA glue is an extra step, but is often well worth the time in reducing problems that occur with hidden defects.

After the blank has been drilled and allowed to cool, wet the inside of the drilled hole with thin CA glue by placing a few drops into the hole and spreading the glue around until the inside is covered. By capillary action the thin glue will be pulled into the defects and hairline cracks. After the glue has dried, test the hole with a clean brass tube to see if the tube will move in and out freely. If the tube is blocked by excess glue you will need to ream or redrill the hole. After you have tested or redrilled the hole, the blank is ready for the tube to be glued in place. The CA glue will reinforce the material where it needs it most: the area immediately surrounding the brass tube.

THE POTATO TRICK

When gluing the tube in a pen blank it is important to line the inside of the pen blank hole with gap-filling glue prior to inserting the tube. Unfortunately, when this is done, as the tube is pushed into the hole, excess glue is often forced into the tube itself. One problem often associated with cleaning and trimming a pen blank using a barrel trimmer is the presence of this excess glue inside the tube. Excess glue takes additional time to remove from the tube and if it is not completely removed, it may cause the wood to crack as the pen is assembled.

One practice that prevents excess glue from getting inside the tube is to seal the end of the tube prior to inserting it into the blank. To do this cut a slice of raw potato about ¼in (6mm) thick and press the tube into the potato, forming a plug at one end (see Fig 9.21). After applying adhesive to the

FIG 9.20 *The tube on the left is dark, showing the effects of oxidation. The oxidation can be removed quickly with abrasive paper.*

FIG 9.21 *The potato plug in the end of the tube prevents glue from entering the tube as it is inserted into the pen blank.*

inside of the blank, press the tube, potato end first, into the blank. The potato plug prevents the excess glue from entering the inside of the tube. The plug will be removed during the trimming process. This method works very well for polyurethane adhesives and epoxies but is not recommended for use with CA adhesives, since the moisture in the potato can quickly accelerate the curing of CA glue and interfere with pressing the tube into the blank.

GLUING INTO PLASTICS

Polyurethane glues are an excellent choice for gluing plastics because of their flexibility and gap-filling qualities. But most polyurethane glues require some moisture in order to activate the curing process. Even 'dry' wood naturally contains the small

FIG 9.22   Water can be used to help activate the curing of polyurethane adhesives on synthetic materials.

FIG 9.23   A hand-held barrel trimmer and a trimmer mounted in an electric hand drill.

amount of moisture needed when using polyurethane glues. However, synthetic materials may not contain this needed moisture. As a result, when using polyurethane glues, it may be helpful to submerse the drilled blanks into water just before gluing (see Fig 9.22).

Next, apply the glue to the inside of the blank and the outside of the tube, and press the tube into the blank. Polyurethane glues require a longer drying period than other glues. Make sure to read the manufacturer's

recommendations for directions and curing times. If in doubt, we recommend allowing polyurethane adhesive to cure overnight.

CYANOACRYLATE ADHESIVE

Cyanoacrylate is a favorite adhesive among pen-makers for gluing the brass tube into the blank. It sets very quickly and the pen can be turned within a matter of minutes. Occasionally, however, CA glues act too fast and set up even before you can push the tube all the way into the blank. Natural substances in some woods such as cocobolo, and also moisture in wood, can actually function as accelerators for CA glue. Heat from drilling can also cause CA glue to set almost immediately. Allowing the blanks to cool down after drilling will usually eliminate this problem. If necessary, an hour or so in the refrigerator will cool the blanks, allowing plenty of working time while gluing in the brass tube with CA glue.

CLEANING AND TRIMMING

Properly cleaning the inside of the tube and trimming the tube square and flush with the end of the blank are crucial to producing a quality pen. When pen kits were first introduced, barrel trimmers were not available. Trimming was done by trying to sand the end of the blank square with the tube using a disc or belt sander. The results were often less than satisfactory, since the drilled hole was not always parallel to the exterior of the blank. When the pen was assembled, unsightly gaps were seen between the ends of the barrels and the metal components of the pen. The introduction of the barrel trimmer has eliminated those frustrations and we consider the barrel trimmer to be essential for consistently producing quality pens.

The barrel trimmer simultaneously cleans the inside of the tube and trims the end. The barrel trimmer can be secured into a simple handle and powered by hand, or mounted in a hand drill or drill press (see Fig 9.23). While being trimmed, the blank can be clamped in a bench vise, or held by the same methods used to secure the blank while drilling, such as the gate jig or the Quick-Grip clamp.

BARREL TRIMMER DIAMETERS

Reducing the diameter of the barrel trimmer head to approximately match the exterior diameter of the finished pen is a trick used by production pen-turners to reduce the time required for trimming pen blanks. It

FIG 9.24 *Grinding a barrel trimmer down to a smaller diameter.*

saves time by reducing the amount of wood to be trimmed and the pressure required to press the trimmer into the wood. The diameter of the cutter head of the trimmer is reduced by mounting the trimmer in a power hand drill and lightly touching the rotating trimmer to a rotating grinding wheel (see Fig 9.24).

The trimmer head should be ground so that it is just slightly larger than the diameter of the pen bushing. Figure 9.25 shows three different diameters of barrel trimmers. The small trimmer in the right of the picture was ground specifically for trimming the standard twist pen.

SHARPENING THE BARREL TRIMMER

Over time, the cutter head of the trimmer will need to be sharpened. This can be done with a medium grit, flat diamond hone. Clamp the trimmer in a bench vise or mount it in the chuck of a hand drill (switched off) so that it can be held securely by hand, then file the front of each of the

FIG 9.25 *Barrel trimmers can be purchased or modified for a specific diameter.*

four faces. Take long, even strokes with the hone. Five or six strokes on each face should restore the edge (see Fig 9.26).

ADAPTING BARREL TRIMMERS

Most barrel trimmers are made to be used with a 7mm pen tube. However, some pens, such as rollerballs and fountain pens, require larger tubes. For these pens an adapter sleeve for the barrel trimmer will need to be made or purchased (see Fig 9.27).

Wooden adapter sleeves are fairly easy to make yourself. To make a wood adapter,

FIG 9.28   A barrel trimmer with interchangeable pilots can be used on pen tubes of varying diameters.

you will need a good hardwood blank glued onto a 7mm brass pen tube. Mount the blank on the lathe just like a regular pen blank. Measure the inside diameter of the larger tube that needs to be trimmed and turn the wood to this measurement. Remove the blank from the lathe and test the fit by sliding it inside the larger tube. The adapter tube should slide inside the larger tube easily, but not allow any slop. This same method can be used to adapt a barrel trimmer for a brass tube with a stepped diameter as discussed in Chapter 5 and pictured in Figure 5.9.

In addition to buying or making adapter sleeves, there is yet another option. Some pen suppliers carry a barrel trimmer kit that consists of one cutting head with interchangeable pilots for pen tubes of different diameters (see Fig 9.28).

FIG 9.26   Honing a barrel trimmer.

FIG 9.27   An adapter sleeve allows a standard 7mm barrel trimmer to be used when trimming pen blanks with larger diameter tubes. This metal adapter sleeve can be purchased from pen suppliers.

CLEANING WITH A DRILL BIT

Before barrel trimmers came along, the insides of the tubes were cleaned of excess glue by using a drill bit. A 'D'-size drill bit is the exact size needed for the inside diameter of the standard 7mm pen tube (see Fig 9.29). Occasionally, excess glue may be particularly tenacious and difficult to remove using a barrel trimmer. This is particularly true of the polyurethane glues. A drill bit of the appropriate diameter can be used to chase out any stubborn glue left behind by the barrel trimmer.

FIG 9.29 *Using a D-size drill bit, secured in a wooden handle, to ream excess glue from inside a pen tube.*

FIG 9.30 *Using a countersink bit to chamfer the inside end of a pen tube.*

CHAMFERING TO REDUCE CRACKING

Sometimes the finished exterior material of a pen may crack during assembly. This is often caused by an excessively tight fit between the end of the tube and the metal tip or cap of the pen. The likelihood of this problem occurring can be reduced by chamfering the inside corner of each end of the tubes (see Fig 9.30). This removes any burrs created while trimming, and slightly relieves the press fit between the tube and the adjoining part.

TECHNIQUES FOR TURNING PENS

In general, standard turning techniques can be employed when turning pens. However, based on the various working properties of different materials, we offer here a few specific suggestions of how to use the tools in various situations.

ROUGH TURNING USING A GOUGE

We generally recommend first using a gouge to rough the blanks down to within about ⅛in (3mm) of the final diameter. The gouge can be used in a variety of ways to accomplish this. We will discuss three specific approaches, either of which may be preferred depending on the working properties of the wood or other material being turned.

The first method is to begin the cut at one end of the blank and continue the cut through the full length of the piece (see Fig 9.31). This method is similar in fashion to the most common method of roughing spindles and works best for woods that are rather straight in grain direction. This cut can be made rather aggressively and will yield good results on woods that are relatively easy to work with.

The second method is also very aggressive and is recommended for woods that may have varying grain patterns and be more difficult for general turning. Here we take several successive short, deep cuts, each feeding toward the center of the axis rather than along the axis (see Fig 9.32).

FIG 9.31 *Roughing using long continuous strokes is quick and efficient when turning straight-grained stock.*

FIG 9.32 *When roughing, short strokes reduce the chance of major tearout.*

With this approach there is less likelihood of lifting off a large chunk of irregular grain, particularly near the end of the pen blank, which sometimes happens when using long, continuous cuts.

The third technique for roughing is one that we recommend whenever using woods that are particularly difficult to turn without tearing. This could include woods such as some stabilized burls, Dymondwood that is cut on a bias to the grain, and dense hardwoods with angled, curly, or otherwise irregular grain. This method calls for first reducing the diameter of the blank at each end to the point where it is only about $^1\!/_{16}$in (1–2mm) over the desired final diameter. This cut is made by rolling the flute of the gouge slightly toward the blank, feeding it into the end of the blank and then toward the outer diameter (see Fig 9.33).

This is an 'uphill' cut, or in other words cutting from small to large diameter, and is contrary to the conventional wisdom of always cutting 'downhill' or from large to small diameter. We recommend an uphill cut on very difficult woods because it first removes the unsupported wood at the end of the blank that would otherwise be most likely to blow out when cutting toward the end of the blank.

Notice, in Fig 9.34, that the wood at the end of the blank broke away, exposing the brass tube inside. This problem can usually be avoided by first removing the wood at

FIG 9.34   An example of what sometimes occurs when cutting irregularly grained wood from one end to the other.

FIG 9.35   After the pen blank has been roughed down, it can be reduced to the final shape and diameter using a 'pull' cut.

each end as pictured in Fig 9.33. Once the ends of the blank have been removed, the middle sections can be removed using either of the first two roughing methods.

FINISH TURNING USING A GOUGE

After the bulk of the wood is removed during the roughing process, there are again various methods that can be used to make the final cleaning passes. The finish passes can be made either with a gouge or with a skew. If the gouge is used, we recommend trying the following two variations. The first we refer to as a 'pull' cut (see Fig 9.35). This cut is made by rolling the flute slightly toward the wood, and while leading with the handle, dragging the cutting edge from one end to the other. The cutting action of this cut is partially scraping and partially shearing, but perhaps more scraping than shearing. This cut has the advantage of

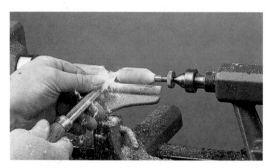

FIG 9.33   By first removing the wood at each end of the blank, the possibility of the blank tearing out at the end is reduced. This method is not recommended for straight-grained wood.

FIG 9.36 *Making a finish cut using the shearing technique with a shallow gouge. Notice the shining surface of the freshly cut wood directly behind the cutting edge of the gouge.*

being relatively easy to control, but has the disadvantage of not producing as fine a surface as other finishing cuts.

For a more refined finish cut with the gouge, try using a 'push' cut, where the bevel of the tool rides the wood just behind the cutting edge. Here you push the tool forward with the cutting edge leading the way. This is a true shearing cut, which should produce a shiny, clean surface (see Fig 9.36). This cut is more difficult to control, but can be learned with appropriate practice.

FINISH TURNING WITH A SKEW
Finish cuts can also be made using a skew. The skew is generally more difficult to control than the gouge, but, once mastered, will produce the finest of results. We offer four different approaches to using a skew for finish turning a pen.

The first of these, shearing while leading with the heel of the skew, is perhaps the most traditional (see Fig 9.37). This cut yields excellent results but requires a relatively high level of skill. Here the bevel is in contact with the wood and the cut produces a fine, almost polished surface. As with shearing using a gouge, this cut is also classified as a 'push' cut. The shavings exiting the wood should be fine curls.

The second cut is shearing while leading with the toe of the skew (see Fig 9.38). This cut is a slight modification on the first and

incorporates the same basic principles. Here, as with the previous cut, the skew is pushed forward with the cutting edge leading and the bevel rubbing on the wood just behind the cut. Notice, though, that the toe, or long point of the skew, is leading the way.

The techniques for shearing with a skew while leading with the heel or leading with the toe are very similar; and both should produce a good, clean cut. Most people do prefer one method over the other. However, this preference may often simply be due to whichever technique they were first introduced to and first become comfortable with. We recommend you develop some level of skill with both approaches before deciding to abandon either. Although these two cuts are very similar, they are both useful to know how to do.

A third technique for producing finish cuts using a skew can be described as 'planing' or 'shear-peeling'. This cut is a subtle variation of the tool angle used in shearing with the toe of the skew. With this cut the cutting edge of the tool is kept almost parallel to the horizontal axis of the

FIG 9.37 *Shearing with the heel of the skew.*

FIG 9.38 *Shearing with the toe of the skew.*

FIG 9.39 The cutting edge contacts the wood between the 10 o'clock and 11 o'clock position as viewed from the tailstock of the lathe. If the fingers of the left hand are brought underneath the toolrest and held gently against the rotating stock, the cut is easier to control and the fingers give an immediate reading as to the quality of the cut.

wood (parallel to the toolrest), and the cutting edge rides high on the stock being cut (see Fig 9.39).

The final finish cut using a skew is very handy for working with materials that chip and tear easily. This cut is best described as a 'shear-scrape' cut. This is not an aggressive cut, as it removes a very small amount of wood. However, the cut is quite easy to control and usually produces good results on even the most difficult woods. Shear-scraping with a skew is also very useful when working synthetics such as alternative ivory and Corian. Here we lead with neither the toe nor the heel of the skew, but rather the lower center section of the cutting edge. The shaft of the skew is positioned almost perpendicular to the toolrest and angled back about 45°. The tool is then dragged lightly along the wood, contacting the work at about the 9:00–9:30 position as viewed from the tailstock (see Fig 9.40).

TOOL SIZES

Standard size turning tools tend to be somewhat large and cumbersome when turning pens. On the other hand, many types of 'miniature' turning tools have blades that are too small in diameter or too thin in cross section to allow the turner to

work with any amount of force. We have found mid-size tools that are a little larger than standard miniature tools to be ideal. We recommend tools with handles about 9in (230mm) in length, and blade lengths of around 4in (100mm). The blades should be heavy enough to resist vibration and chatter when taking heavy cuts.

Tools of this size are comfortable to use and allow you to work close to the wood, giving good control and a nice feel of the cut as it takes place. These medium-small tools allow the turner to take aggressive cuts as well as very fine cuts. In addition, with a little practice, when using relatively small tools, both a gouge and a skew can be held simultaneously, eliminating the time required to set a tool down and pick up another (see Fig 9.41).

USE ONLY SHARP TOOLS

Keep your tools sharp. Sharp tools make turning more efficient and more enjoyable.

FIG 9.40 Shear-scraping with a skew chisel.

FIG 9.41 When using smaller tools, both a gouge and a skew can be held in one hand, increasing efficiency in a production situation.

FIG 9.42 *The wood on these finished pens cracked. Heat-sensitive woods require special precautions, and the finished pens must be kept free from exposure to an overheated environment.*

You may be doing everything else correctly, but if your tool is dull, trying to turn wood is an exercise in frustration. As a rule of thumb, if you think the tool might be dull, chances are it is. Take the time to sharpen it before continuing.

LATHE SPEED

When turning pens and pencils, keep the lathe speed high – around 3,000–3,500rpm. This will reduce the time required to remove the material during the roughing stage, and will produce a finer surface during the finishing stage.

WORKING WITH DIFFICULT WOODS

Some of the most beautiful woods for pens are often quite difficult to work with. This is especially true of decayed or spalted woods, very dense exotic woods, burls with natural defects and Dymondwood. The properties of these woods, along with suggestions for working them, have been covered; here are a few additional tips related to working with woods that are particularly sensitive to heat, woods with soft/punky areas, and woods that contain natural voids.

HEAT-SENSITIVE WOODS

Heat-sensitive woods like the ebonies, blackwood, snakewood and pink ivory will often develop cracks even after the pen blank has been turned. This is almost certain to happen if the finished pen is exposed to the warm sun or left in a hot car during the summertime (see Fig 9.42).

Heat-sensitive woods require extra care during the drilling, gluing and finishing processes. As you work with these materials, pay extra attention to the following points:

- Check to see if the wood is dry: it should be under 10% moisture content before working.
- During the drilling process keep the drill bit sharp and cool to prevent overheating the blank.
- After drilling the blanks, set them aside and allow them to stabilize for a few days. Reinforce the inside of the blank with thin CA glue. Test the hole with a brass tube to check for wood movement and redrill the hole if necessary.
- Rough up the outside of the brass tube with sandpaper before gluing.
- Glue both the inside of the hole and the outside of the tube using polyurethane glue.
- Finally, when sanding and finishing, use a light touch so as not to build up too much heat.

FIG 9.43 Stabilizing soft, punky wood by applying thin CA prior to making the finish cuts.

SOFT AND PUNKY WOODS

To stabilize a pen blank containing pockets of punky wood, select the soft areas and apply thin cyanoacrylate. The punky wood will soak up the CA glue like a sponge. Once the glue has cured you may drill the blank. After drilling, flood the punky wood inside the hole with thin CA glue. After the glue inside the hole has set, test the hole with a brass tube to ensure that the hole has not become blocked with glue. If the hole is clogged, redrill the hole, then glue in a tube and barrel trim the blank and tube.

Mount the blank on the lathe and rough turn it to ^{1}/8in (3mm) larger than the diameter of the bushing. Stop the lathe and inspect the punky sections for tearout and unsaturated areas. Reapply the thin CA glue to the areas where the glue has not penetrated thoroughly (see Fig 9.43). Take another pass, turning the blank to ^{1}/16in (2mm) larger than the finished diameter. Stop the lathe and again inspect for punky areas. Apply more CA glue if necessary. Make a finishing pass to the desired final size and shape. Again, check for unsaturated portions and apply more CA glue if needed. If the soft wood is not adequately stabilized, it will sand unevenly, leaving an unsightly depression in the surface of the finished pen.

DEALING WITH DEFECTS IN WOOD

Some of the most beautiful pen woods commonly contain natural defects such as small voids, bark pockets, pin knots and worm holes. Burls will often have small cracks that curve with the grain of the burl. These defects present interesting challenges to the pen-maker. When using such wood, you are faced with three options. One option is to ignore the defects. Another is to hide them. The third option is to highlight them. Generally speaking, the pen will be more successful if the defects are either hidden or highlighted, rather than ignored.

Hiding Defects

Small voids and cracks can be hidden effectively when filled with a combination of matching sanding dust and thin cyanoacrylate (see Fig 9.44). When voids show up, first turn the pen blank to within about ^{1}/16in (2mm) of the final diameter. Then remove the toolrest and sand lightly from the underneath side of the wood, catching the sanding dust as it falls on the sandpaper. Place some thin CA glue in the void and immediately pack it with the sanding dust.

FIG 9.44 The void in this English brown oak burl can be filled with sanding dust and thin CA glue.

FIG 9.45 The void in the oak burl after being repaired with sanding dust and CA glue.

Next, saturate the area with thin CA glue, adding more sanding dust if needed. Build the area up until the void is completely filled and slightly over size. Once the adhesive has cured, turn away the excess material using a sharp tool and finishing cuts. Then sand and finish the pen (see Fig 9.45).

Highlighting Defects

To highlight the defective area a contrasting filler is used. Defects can be highlighted with a number of fillers, such as powdered gemstones, colored epoxy, and metal shavings. The procedure for each is very similar and is accomplished in essentially the same manner as hiding the defects, described above. The primary difference is that when highlighting defects a contrasting material is inlaid in the void rather than using matching sawdust. Black stain concentrate in powdered form works particularly well on burls, since it appears somewhat like a natural bark pocket (see Figs 9.46 and 9.47).

Brass shavings provide an interesting contrast when used with darker woods. Brass shavings should be avoided on light-colored woods due to the fact that the brass stains the wood during sanding. Crushed gemstones offer a variety of natural yet colorful options for inlay. Some of the more popular stones include turquoise, coral, malachite, chrysacola and abalone.

SANDING WITH MICRO-MESH

Micro-Mesh is a cushioned abrasive that produces a very fine and uniform scratch pattern. Unlike common sandpaper, where the abrasive grit is locked at irregular heights and at random angles, Micro-Mesh allows the abrasive grit to move and depress to a common level (see Fig 9.48). As the cushioning abrasive is moved across the surface, the abrasive grit is rotated slightly to cut with a smooth shaving action. This results in a uniform scratch pattern that produces a very fine finish in fewer steps.

FIG 9.46 Here a small pin knot became separated from the wood, exposing the brass tube.

FIG 9.47 The pin knot hole was highlighted using black stain concentrate and CA glue. The repair looks much like other pin knots on the pen that remained intact as the pen was turned.

FIG 9.48 Sanding with Micro-Mesh.

For plastic-based material such as Dymondwood, Crushed Velvet, celluloid acetate and others, when sanding with Micro-Mesh, often no finish is required at all. You can simply stop sanding when you reach the desired sheen. Micro-Mesh can be used wet or dry. To produce a satin finish sand up to 3600 grit. A high gloss finish will appear by sanding through 6000 to 12000.

Sanding with Micro-Mesh is similar to the procedure described in previous chapters. First sand up to 320 grit with conventional sandpaper. Then, using a light touch, begin sanding with 1500 Micro-Mesh wrapped around the foam pad, and sand until all of the 320 grit scratches are gone. Continue to sand with the Micro-Mesh, ranging through 1800, 2400, 3200, 3600, 4000, 6000, 8000 and 12000 grit. You can stop at any point during sanding when you are satisfied with the finish. When finishing wood with a French polish, sand as described above up to 3200 grit.

Stop after you reach 3200, and apply the French polish to the pen barrels. Begin sanding again with 2400 grit and work to finer grits, stopping when you have the desired finish. As the cloth begins to load, it can be cleaned by rapping it against the palm of your hand, or it can be brushed with a stiff, short-bristle brush.

FIG 9.49 Having all the necessary parts organized and at hand helps increase the efficiency of assembly. This storage case includes components for twist pens finished in shiny gold, matte gold and matte nickel.

FIG 9.50 To make a simple clip-and-cap assembly tube, drill a hole partially through a piece of wood, insert a pen tube so that about 3/8in (10mm) of the end of the tube is exposed, then use a hacksaw to cut a slit in the end of the tube.

ASSEMBLY

Efficiency and accuracy while assembling pens depends largely on how well the pen parts are organized and the use of a few simple assembly aids. In order to keep pen parts, drills and bushings in order, a storage case is very helpful. Look for a box with adjustable dividers that can be arranged to fit your particular needs (see Fig 9.49).

On rare occasions, the pen kit may have defective parts. This may include any number of things, such as scratches in the plating, bent clips, small burrs on machined parts, and more. By inspecting the parts prior to assembly, you may save yourself the frustration of having to disassemble a completed pen because of a faulty component. Most suppliers are very good at replacing defective parts upon request.

PRE-ASSEMBLING THE CLIP AND CAP

Pen and pencil clips often cause problems during assembly. It can be quite awkward to hold the pen cap, pen clip and finished barrel in one hand and operate the vise with the other. To help with this problem you can pre-assemble the cap and clip. Start by cutting a 3/8in (10mm) long slit on one end of an extra pen tube with a hacksaw blade, or grind a slit using a grinder (see Fig 9.50).

The slit in the brass tube will allow the clip and cap to be pressed into the slit end of the tube, but will also release it after it is assembled. To pre-assemble the cap and clip, set the cap inside the ring of the clip, align them over the slit end of the assembly tube, then use a mallet to tap the cap into the tube. This presses the clip firmly onto the cap. The cap and clip assembly can then be slid out of the slitted tube, ready to be pressed into a finished pen barrel (see Fig 9.51).

METHODS FOR PEN ASSEMBLY

Pressing the pen parts together is a very critical step in pen-making. It requires accuracy combined with force in order to get good results. There are several ways to press the parts together. One method is to use a standard bench vise with wood jaws as was used in Chapter 3. The bench vise does a very good job and is perhaps the most common method used.

A second method, handy when you do not have a bench vise available, is to use a Quick-Grip clamp in the same manner as a bench vise. Another method is to use a drill press with a bolt mounted in the drill chuck as a ram for pressing the parts together. (The motor on the drill press, of course, would not be running at the time.) This method can be particularly efficient if combined with the use of a pen press jig as described earlier.

Finally, a small arbor press also works well for pen assembly (see Fig 9.52). The arbor press and drill press operate essentially in the same manner. If you decide to acquire an arbor press for assembling pens, be sure to get a press that has at least 5in (127mm) capacity, otherwise it may not be large enough for assembling a variety of types of pens and pencils.

THE PEN PRESS JIG

A pen press jig helps greatly in the assembly of almost all pens and pencils. It holds the parts at a right angle to the table and provides a flat surface for the parts to register against. No guesswork is needed when setting the pen mechanism. The pen

FIG 9.51 *The cap and clip can be pre-assembled using a pen tube with a slit on one end, and a mallet. A cut stocking has been placed over the large end of the mallet to protect the plating on the cap from the hardwood mallet.*

FIG 9.52 *Using an arbor press is one method that works well for pen assembly.*

assembly jig allows for fast, easy and accurate assembly for one pen as well as hundreds (see Fig 9.53).

The pen assembly jig is very easy to make and use. To use the jig, start by chucking the ram bolt up into the drill chuck as far as it will go and tighten the chuck. Then place the pen press board on the drill press table. Lay out the pen parts according to the supplier's drawings. Match the wood grain of the barrels as you are laying the parts out. Place the lower barrel, tip end up, on the first pin, and the upper barrel cap end up on the second pin. Place the transmission into a hole in the pen press jig with the brass end up. Now you are ready to begin pressing the parts together. Place the pen tip into the top of the barrel and press it into place. (see Fig 9.54).

Next, press the clip and cap into the upper barrel in the same way (see Fig 9.55). Finally, using a v-block as a depth stop, press the open end of the lower barrel onto the brass end of the transmission until the ram bolt contacts the v-block (see Fig 9.56).

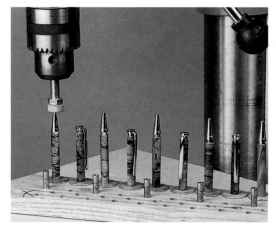

FIG 9.54 The drill press can be used to quickly press the separate pen parts together. Here a pen press jig is used to hold the pen barrels upright while the pen tip is pressed into place.

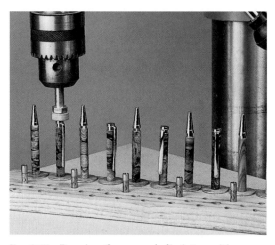

FIG 9.55 Pressing the cap and clip into position.

FIG 9.56 After the tip has been pressed into the barrel, the transmission can be pressed into place. Notice the stop block is used to establish the correct depth when pressing in the transmission.

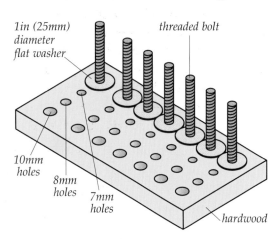

1in (25mm) diameter flat washer

threaded bolt

10mm holes

8mm holes

7mm holes

hardwood

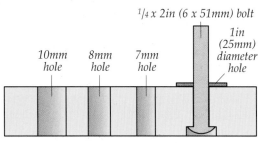

¹/₄ x 2in (6 x 51mm) bolt

10mm hole

8mm hole

7mm hole

1in (25mm) diameter hole

FIG 9.53 The pen press jig.

TROUBLESHOOTING

Pen parts are designed to go together with a press fit and should not require glue to keep them together. However, occasionally parts are a bit loose and need to be secured. To accomplish this, use a toothpick to place a small amount of gap-filling CA or epoxy around the inside of the tube and press the parts together (see Fig 9.57). Never apply glue to the outside of the parts being glued, as it may be pressed out onto the finished exterior of the pen.

Something that can be quite frustrating is when the assembled clip end of a twist pen is stuck onto the transmission, preventing the two halves of the pen from being separated. This happens occasionally when there is some glue residue remaining inside the tube that fits over the transmission. This makes changing a refill difficult and rather unpleasant. To prevent this problem, apply a film of paste wax to the inside of the tube before assembling the two sections of the pen. A cotton swab dipped in paste wax will do the job nicely (see Fig 9.58).

DISASSEMBLY

Sooner or later, anyone who is making several pens will have a need to disassemble one to make a repair or replace a damaged part. It should be emphasized that a much better option to disassembling a

FIG 9.58 *To prevent an excessively tight fit between the transmission and the removable barrel, apply a small amount of paste wax inside the pen tube.*

pen for repairs is to assemble the pen correctly in the first place. It is not always possible to disassemble a pen without destroying one or more parts. Unfortunately, however, it is very easy to make a slight error in assembly or have something go unexpectedly amiss.

Pen disassembly allows you to make repairs, refinish barrels, or replace parts without damaging the other parts. The standard 7mm twist pen and the rollerball pen are relatively simple to take apart using a commercially produced disassembly kit (see Fig 9.59). Pens with threaded couplers, bushings, trim rings and other thin-walled

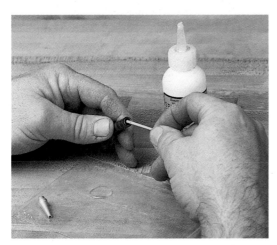

FIG 9.57 *Apply glue to the inside of a tube to secure a loose-fitting pen tip into place.*

FIG 9.59 *This kit, available from pen kit suppliers, is designed for disassembling the parts of the standard twist pen.*

parts are very difficult to disassemble. These types of pens and parts will be damaged, if not destroyed, by taking them apart. Most pen suppliers sell the individual parts for all the pens they carry.

Following are the basic procedures for disassembling a standard twist pen. Using similar concepts and a little ingenuity, you can develop variations of this process to disassemble parts of pens other than this standard pen.

FIG **9.60**   *Removing the clip from the upper barrel.*

- Separate the two halves of the pen by simply pulling them apart by hand.
- Insert the large diameter rod into the open end of the barrel containing the clip. While firmly holding onto the barrel, tap the end of the rod with a mallet to force the clip out of the barrel. It may take several firm taps to remove the clip (see Fig 9.60).
- Remove the refill and insert the small diameter rod through the transmission in the lower barrel and tap the rod to push the tip out of the barrel (see Fig 9.61).
- Finally, insert the exposed end of the transmission into the large, hollow transmission receiver with the taper toward the barrel, then insert the large rod into the other end of the barrel. Press the pieces together in a vise, or set the flat end of the transmission receiver on a solid surface and tap the rod with a mallet. The transmission will be forced out of the barrel and into the receiver. The pen parts should all be in good condition and ready to be used again (see Fig 9.62).

FIG **9.61**   *Removing the tip from the lower barrel.*

FIG **9.62**   *Using the large rod and the transmission receiver to remove the transmission from the barrel.*

CHAPTER 10

WHAT TO DO WITH ALL THESE PENS?

MARKETING

Once you have made your first pen and start to show it to friends and family, you will soon start to hear questions like, 'Did you really make that?', 'Could you make me one?' (One thing you will find out about making pens is that you can give away as many as you may care to make.) Or you may be asked, 'This is beautiful; do you have any I could buy?' It may be that you have no interest whatsoever in selling your pens and only plan to make them for your own use and to give to friends and family as gifts. That is a rewarding option in itself

if you have the expendable time and money required to continue.

If you are like most people, however, unless you are independently wealthy and unusually philanthropic, you will soon grow weary and poor from continually handing out pens as gifts and will need to consider whether you should start charging for them. This is also a positive and rewarding option, as you will most likely discover that turning pens can be quite addictive due to the fun and satisfaction received. Like many, before long you will begin to ask yourself, 'What to do with all these pens?' If so, consider marketing your pens at some level. If nothing else, by selling a few pens, you at least have a hobby that supports itself rather than a hobby that is a financial drain like many often are.

One of the reasons turned pens are such a marketable woodworking project is that writing instruments are truly a consumable item. In order to be considered both consumable and marketable, a project must meet some basic qualifications. Consider the following questions in relation to pens as a marketable product: Is there demand for the product? Yes, almost everyone uses pens on a daily basis. Is the product consumable? Yes, most adults own many pens and pens need to be replaced often; they wear out with use and easily just get lost or misplaced. Does the product have an important function or purpose? Yes, pens are a basic instrument of communication.

The consumable qualities of pens make them a natural product for sales, and most pen-makers will find opportunities for sales whether they seek them or not. Selling your pens can become almost as much fun as making them. This idea of selling a product can bring new excitement as well as a little extra money. Do not let the word 'sales' scare you off. You can charge as much or as little as you want. You may decide to sell the pen for the cost of the kit and the wood with the intention simply to cover your costs. It is a lot of fun to sell something you have made no matter what you want to charge or how many you make.

POCKET PEN SELLING

One of the first forms of selling your pens is to show your pen to everyone you meet. We call this method of selling 'pocket pen selling'. The pocket pen salesperson will carry two or three pens and pencils and have them available to use and to show others whenever the opportunity arises. These pens will be the newest and brightest and may even be conspicuously placed to stick above the pocket far enough to show off the wood. This opportunist pen-maker is always prepared with pen in hand whenever someone asks the inevitable question, 'Does anyone have a pen?'

The pocket pen salesperson is proud of his or her creation, and rightly should be! If you look close enough you may see a smile from ear to ear as the pen is placed in your hand. His motto will be that everyone needs one or two more pens. This method of selling pens is often as far as the hobbyist may venture into pen sales, or it may be the natural starting point for you to move on to other more formal types of marketing.

CRAFT SHOWS

Local and small craft shows can offer you an excellent first chance at retailing your goods (see Fig 10.2). Craft shows allow the maker to have full control over the selling

FIG 10.2 Many pen-makers find craft shows to be an excellent venue for marketing their turned pens. Here is one sample of a pen display for a craft show.

process and provide instant feedback from customers. Talking and interacting with customers can give you a good idea about pricing, displays, selling, customer likes, and interest in your products. Craft shows can range in attendance from 100 people for local craft shows to top-ranked arts and craft shows with over 100,000 people.

The range of craft shows allows you to determine your involvement. Small shows may require little to no booth fees and only a handful of pens displayed on a table, while large, competitive shows will require an expensive display booth with booth fees sometimes costing £500 or more. We recommend selecting shows that require all craftsmen/artists to display original works and handmade items only. When possible, talk to other artists and craftsmen who have participated in various shows. Their recommendations are a valuable source of information. Craft shows offer some of your best chances to sell and interact with customers at a level that you are comfortable with.

Galleries/Gift Shops

Galleries and gift shops can also offer new and interesting opportunities for selling your products. When looking into galleries to sell your products, you need to be very selective in choosing one that represents your work in the most positive light. Do your homework by looking for a gallery that already sells wood items. Also look for a theme of the local area: it should be compatible with handmade wood items. Try to visit the galleries to see if your products and prices compare with existing items. It is also wise to contact other artists already exhibiting in the galleries to find out what type of clientele the gallery attracts, if the gallery pays its artists promptly, and if your pens are likely to do well in the gallery.

After your research is compiled and you have selected a gallery or two, it is time to

contact them. Call to make an appointment with the buyer at the buyer's convenience. Make your first impression your best impression by having in hand a sample of your products, prices, displays, and promotional material. This should include items like business cards, price lists, photographs, display units, and samples. Most galleries will ask new suppliers to work on a commission which is deducted from the retail price. The commission will usually vary from 60/40% (60% to artist) to 50/50% split and is paid only after the item is sold.

To reduce record keeping on small items, many galleries will buy your pens outright. Generally they will purchase a dozen or more pens at wholesale price. When their inventory of your pens begins to get low they will reorder. Make sure to keep in contact with the galleries on a regular basis. This will show your interest in the gallery and give the gallery a chance to reorder your products.

Corporate Sales

Small and large businesses present an excellent sales opportunity for the pen-maker. Businesses will often have a need for reasonably priced gifts that can be used for promotional purposes or as presents for employees at Christmas time or at individual birthdays. Pens are an excellent choice because they can be reasonably priced, have genuine value, and can easily be custom laser engraved for advertising (see Figs 10.3 and 10.4).

When working with a business, call ahead for an appointment to make sure you are talking and meeting with the right person. It is important that you are able to meet with a person who is in a position to make a decision regarding the purchase of promotional items for the company.

By planning ahead, you may ask the buyer key questions during your introductory call, such as the following:

- What is your budget for promotional gifts items?
- Would this be a seasonal purchase?
- Who will receive this gift?
- What are your motives for the gift?

- Will you use the gift for advertising purposes?
- What time of year do you plan to buy?
- What types of gift items have you given in the past?

FIG 10.3 *Pen boxes can be customized by laser engraving with a business logo. Even relatively large or detailed logos will usually fit on a pen box.*

FIG 10.4 *Pens can be customized with company or individual names.*

If questions such as these can be asked before the appointment, it will often make or break the sale. This information will assist you in preparing for your sales presentation. Be on time for your appointment, inform the buyer of anything you think may be helpful to them, be prepared to answer potential questions, then let your sample pens and boxes make the sale. Make sure to follow up the sale or even a missed sale by keeping in contact with the buyer.

THE INTERNET

Although the internet is relatively new as a marketing tool, there are already numerous turners who offer pens for sale over it. The internet has enormous potential due to easy access for buyers from all over the world. Products offered on the internet are usually handled in two ways. One is to have your own web site. This would be similar to having your own retail store. It offers the most control but also requires the highest level of commitment and financial risk.

The other method is to be part of an internet 'mall' in which a group of people are represented by a site manager who takes a commission on all sales. While we have not used the internet to market our work, we are confident that it offers significant opportunities. Perhaps only the future will tell what the internet really has to offer pen-turners who choose to seriously pursue it as a tool for marketing their products.

SELLING POINTS

Capitalize on unique materials and quality craftsmanship. Many of Taiwan's pen suppliers offer finished wood pens. These pens are produced in minutes and do not cost a lot more than the pen kits you can buy to use in making your own pens. While pens mass-produced in Taiwan are generally of good quality, they are limited to generic styles and to plainer woods such as straight-grained maple, cherry and walnut.

Woodturners who produce pens for sale should not try to compete with the mass-produced pens from Taiwan. Most people are willing to pay more for a pen that is carefully handmade by someone they are personally acquainted with, and who took special effort to select unique woods and possibly include some personal touch in the final design. The uniqueness of handmade pens should be used as a key selling point. A handmade pen provides a quality not found in today's mass-produced world.

The wood should be the most attractive part of the pen. Fortunately there are thousands of wonderful woods to choose from. In fact, the availability of the vast variety of woods and other materials that make beautiful pens is a main attraction both for pen-makers and pen collectors. Pride in craftsmanship and the display of the world's most beautiful woods will set your pens apart from the mass-produced pens of Taiwan and other countries.

INFORMATION CARD

Handcrafted pens need to be presented as something special. Many times the pen-maker will be able to relate stories behind the gathering of the wood or the making of the pen. They should supply information such as how the pen was made, the type of wood and why this wood is special, types of refills that may be used in the pen, and perhaps something unique about the maker and his or her distinctive pen designs. This is what will set your pens apart from others.

A simple business card is a great way to inform the pen recipient of this information. The card may include information such as that shown in the example on page 138.

Another way to provide the customer with information regarding your pen is to include a small information card inside a pen box that is included with the pen.

ABOUT THE WOOD

This pen is handcrafted by

_____

from _____wood,

that grows in _____ .

The tree grows to about _____ in diameter

and _____ tall.

The pen was made from a solid piece of wood with the grain oriented to match between the two barrels of the pen. It was hand-turned on a wood lathe. This is one of forty different woods from around the world I use in making my pens.

CARE OF THE WOOD

With use the wood will darken; to clean and restore the gloss simply buff with a high-quality furniture wax.

PLATING

The pen mechanism includes a durable 10 karat gold alloy plating.

REFILL

Gently pull apart the top half of the pen from the lower half to expose the refill. The pen uses a

_____ style pen refill No._____ .

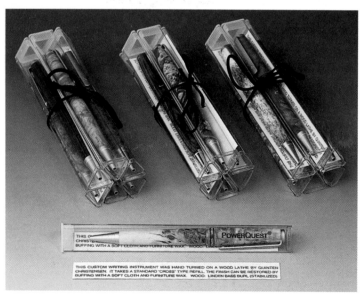

FIG 10.5 An information card can be designed to fit inside almost any type of pen box.

A brief information card can be made to fit almost any type of pen box. Again, this information card can be customized to include a description of the pen and any key information that the maker may want to pass on to the future owner (see Fig 10.5).

DISPLAY BOXES

Whether you are making one or one hundred pens, how you present them will have a significant impact on your success in marketing. In order to show and protect the pen a box or sleeve is often used (see Fig 10.6). Many people buy pens to present as gifts to others. If a pen is given as a gift, it will almost always be given in a display box or storage box of some kind. The pen should be presented with the same effort and style that went into the making of it. The box should protect the pen from premature wear and should add value to it.

While one can make a wood box from matching wood, this often takes more effort and time than it takes to make the pens. While a box is important to the final presentation of the pen, the container should not be perceived to have more value than the pen itself. Most suppliers of pen parts also offer an excellent selection of plastic, fabric and wood boxes at a reasonable price. The wood boxes are usually made from bubinga, maple, or walnut. Wood boxes usually cost a little more than the basic pen kits, but they are well worth the cost! Wood boxes offer the added advantage of being excellent for custom laser engraving of business logos, nature scenes and sports figures.

LASER ENGRAVING

Of the various methods available for customizing pens and pen boxes, perhaps the most versatile and popular is laser engraving (see Fig 10.7). Lasers are a relatively new technology, having been developed during the 1950s. The word 'laser' is an acronym for 'light amplification by stimulated emission of radiation'. A laser is essentially a light source that emits a single color of light with rays that are parallel. Using lenses and mirrors, the rays are focused on a minute area. This concentration of light can be controlled to heat, melt, burn, or vaporize materials in a well-defined area. One distinct advantage of laser heat over other sources of heat is that it does not affect surrounding areas. The only spot affected by the heat is that where the laser beam is focused.

Lasers are tremendously versatile and are widely used in manufacturing, medicine, communication, and other fields. During the past two decades machines for laser engraving have become available and have been adopted by many businesses for the purpose of custom engraving. Recent

FIG 10.6 *A variety of pen boxes. These boxes range quite widely in price.*

technology has made custom laser engraving relatively inexpensive. Names of individuals or businesses can be typed on a computer and downloaded to a laser engraver that quickly burns the name on pens and pen boxes. Business logos,

FIG 10.7 *Pen display boxes, with laser engraving such as these wildlife scenes, are available from some suppliers that carry pen kits.*

Fig 10.8 A customized pen box and pen.

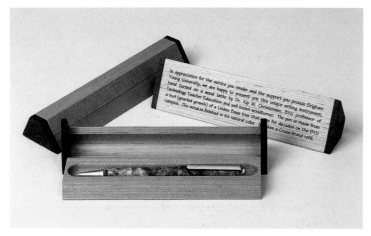

Fig 10.9 An example of how a pen box can be customized to include a special message of appreciation.

profit. Pens are usually engraved after the pen is finished and assembled. Generally, no additional work is required after engraving except for cleaning off a small amount of smoke residue from the area surrounding the engraving. This is done by using a slightly damp cloth followed by wiping with a dry cloth.

Laser engraving is quick, clean, quite inexpensive, and permanent. Customized engraving can add value and meaning to pens, particularly those presented as gifts. A custom engraved pen and pencil set presented in an engraved wood box makes a handsome and valued gift.

Businesses that do custom laser engraving can be found in most cities. Quite often the major products for these businesses are trophies and custom-made plaques. The cost of custom laser engraving can vary widely depending on the quantity of a particular image to be engraved and the size and complexity of the image. Most companies that do custom engraving require a set-up fee regardless of the quantity to be engraved. Beyond the set-up fee, a quantity price is determined.

HIGHLIGHTING LASER ENGRAVING

How well laser engraved images contrast with the surrounding wood varies significantly from species to species. When most natural woods are engraved, the intense heat from the laser beam scorches the wood and leaves it dark brown or even black. This usually contrasts well with most woods except those that are particularly dark such as ebony and some of the rosewoods. It is interesting, however, that images engraved in stabilized woods generally do not turn dark like those engraved in natural woods. As a result, it is sometimes necessary to darken the engraved image to increase the level of contrast and make the image easier to see.

including line art and half-tones, can be computer scanned, manipulated on screen if desired, transferred to a laser and then engraved (see Fig 10.8). In addition to names and logos, any text, such as a special message, can be engraved on a pen display box (see Fig 10.9).

Laser engravers will etch on almost any material that may be used in pen-making. An exception to this is metal, which is not affected by most laser engravers and some plastics, which may melt rather than engrave cleanly, but wood and antler engrave very nicely.

Customizing pens through laser engraving has opened a huge new sales market to those who make turned pens for

On most woods, engraving can be darkened slightly by simply applying a touch of mineral oil to the engraved area. However, it is often desirable to blacken or even highlight an engraved image with a contrasting color. We have experimented with several methods for darkening and coloring laser-engraved images and have found that acrylic artist paint produces good results. The examples in Fig 10.10 show various laser engraving applications. The top sample is natural box elder burl with engraving that has not been modified in any way. The image is naturally dark brown in color and contrasts well with the surrounding wood. The second sample is stabilized box elder burl. Notice that the engraving on the stabilized wood did not turn dark and does not show up well. The middle sample is stabilized spalted buckeye burl with the engraving highlighted with black acrylic artist paint. Without the addition of the paint, this image would be very difficult to see on the dark wood background. The two bottom samples show engraved stabilized box elder burl, each highlighted with acrylic paint. Note how the paint lends strong contrast with the

FIG 10.10 *Examples of various laser engraving applications.*

wood. To highlight an engraved image with acrylic paint, use a cotton-tip swab to apply a generous amount of paint over the engraved area and immediately remove the excess paint by wiping with a clean cloth (see Fig 10.11). When using paint to darken an image, it is important that the pores in the wood be thoroughly sealed with finish and that there is a good coat of surface finish on the pen. Otherwise, open pores in the wood will trap the paint.

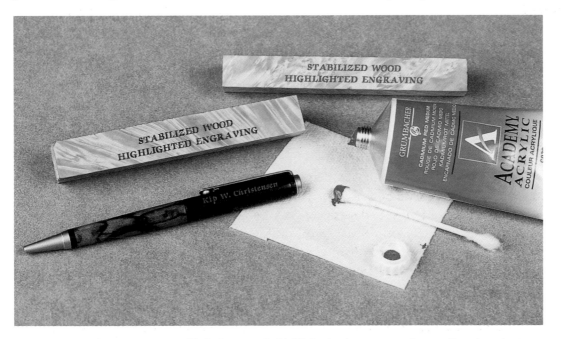

FIG 10.11 *Even laser engraving on black ebony can be highlighted using a contrasting acrylic artist paint.*

GUARANTEES

Most people who buy custom pens will want the pen to be guaranteed to some extent. The most common guarantee is for repair or replacement in case of damaged parts or faulty workmanship. If a pen has faulty parts, such as a transmission that does not function properly, it can simply be disassembled and the defective part replaced. An example of faulty workmanship is when a wood is used that is not fully dry and it cracks within a few days or weeks of the pen being made. Again, the pen can be disassembled and reassembled with newly turned barrels.

Perhaps the most common problem is that of the metal plating wearing off. In one case a pen with cheaper quality plating was returned in less than three weeks with almost all the gold plating worn off. This, however, was an extreme case where the pen was used almost constantly all day. Nevertheless, pen-makers should be aware that the type and quality of plating is an important feature and will most likely influence the type of guarantee they may want to offer. It is recommended that lifetime guarantees are offered only on pens made with platings that also carry a lifetime guarantee from the supplier. This, of course, will significantly affect the cost of the pen components and should be reflected in the selling cost of the finished pen.

As a general rule, the more pens you want to sell the better the guarantee should be, but do not offer a guarantee that you are not prepared to meet.

PRICING

How to price your work is an interesting question that does not have a simple, quick answer. Yet it is a question you may have to answer for yourself a lot sooner than you may think. This may happen with the very first pen you turn when someone asks, 'Can you make one for me?' At that point, you can either give a pen away or make your first sale. How much you charge depends largely on your motives for making pens. In general, an easy and reliable way to find current retail market value is to check local gift shops and galleries that might sell handmade pens. Another option is to ask your pen kit supplier.

Many times pen-makers will develop a wholesale price list based on cost of materials, production costs including overheads, and profit. From the wholesale price a retail price is established. Most retailers will double your wholesale prices. Doubling the wholesale price allows retailers to cover their cost and make a profit as well. Selling your pens directly to a consumer is generally considered making a retail sale and the price should be determined accordingly. When quantities of pens are sold to the same individual, wholesale pricing is generally used.

GALLERY

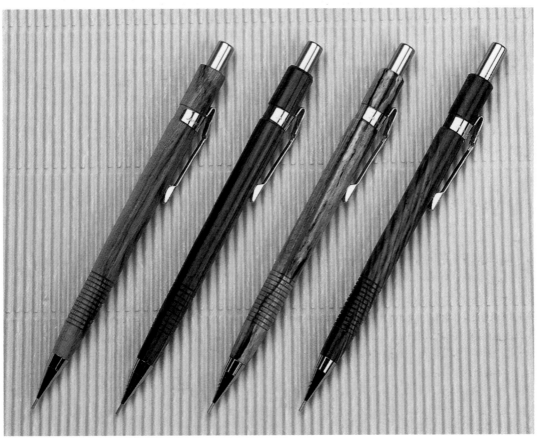

Pencils made using standard Pentel mechanisms, turned by Rex Burningham.
Woods, from left: desert ironwood, cocobolo, spalted maple, cocobolo.

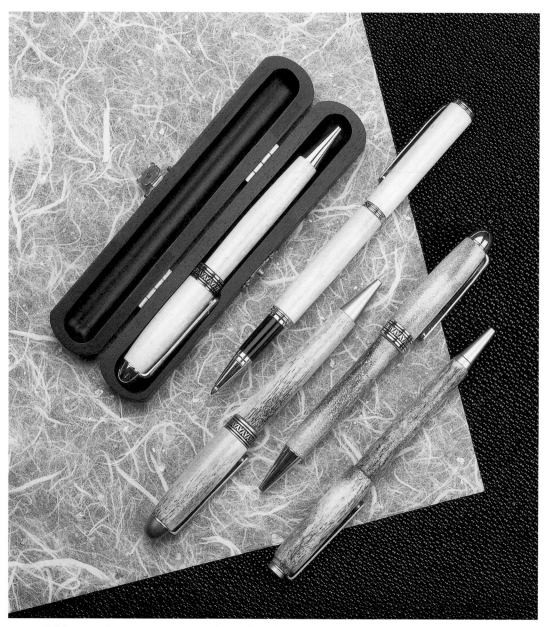

Walrus tusk pen in a custom ebony box by Brian McEvoy, and pens made from deer and elk antler by Rex Burningham and Kip Christensen.

Pens with wood and antler center bands by Rex Burningham and Kip Christensen. Materials, from left: dyed box elder burl and pink ivory, dyed fiddleback maple and dyed maple, spalted buckeye burl and ebony, myrtle and blackwood, box elder burl and pink ivory, spalted buckeye burl and ebony, pink ivory and antler, ebony with spalted English beech and antler.

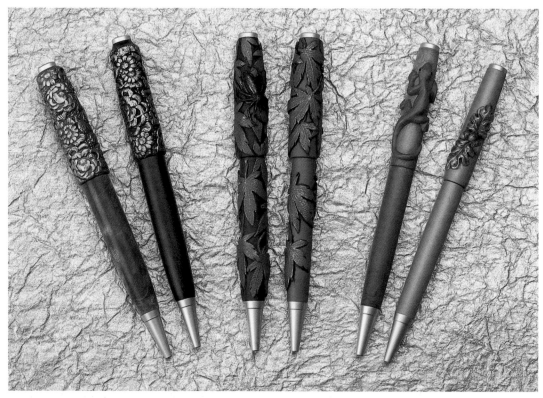

Pens designed and sculpted by polymer clay artist Jacqueline E. Lee.

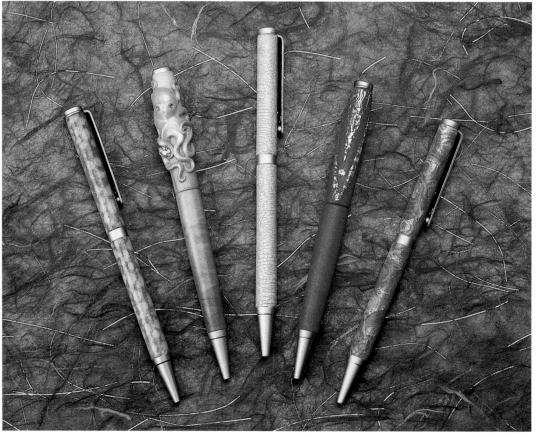

Polymer clay pens by Jacqueline E. Lee.

Custom-designed pens and pencils by Dick Sing. Materials, from left: spalted oak burl, cocobolo with cast polyester, box elder burl, kingwood with cast polyester, fiddleback koa, kingwood with cast polyester, che chen burl.

Fountain pens designed and produced by Rex Burningham. Materials, from left: blackwood, snakewood, pink ivory, box elder burl.

Pens produced using an ornamental milling machine by Tracy Anderson and Kip Christensen. Materials, from left: alternative ivory, cocobolo, blackwood, cocobolo, padauk, Madagascar rosewood.

Straight twist pens produced by Dick Sing using a combination of Dymondwood, Corian and Pickguard.

A pen with spiral fluting by Tracy Anderson, made using an ornamental mill. Alternative ivory. (Photo by Chris Herbert.)

Straight fluting produced by Tracy Anderson on an ornamental milling machine. Western maple burl. (Photo by Chris Herbert.)

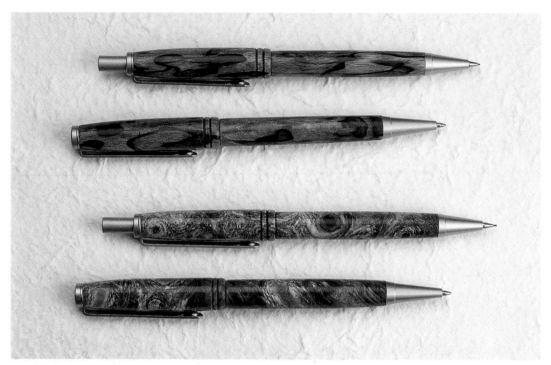

Pen and pencil sets by Kip Christensen, made using the basic twist pen and click pencil kits.
Materials, from top: spalted English beech, spalted buckeye burl.

Pens by Preston Christensen (age 12) made from stabilized and dyed box elder burl.
The light blonde color of box elder burl makes it an excellent wood for dying various colors.
The pen on the far left is natural, all others are dyed.

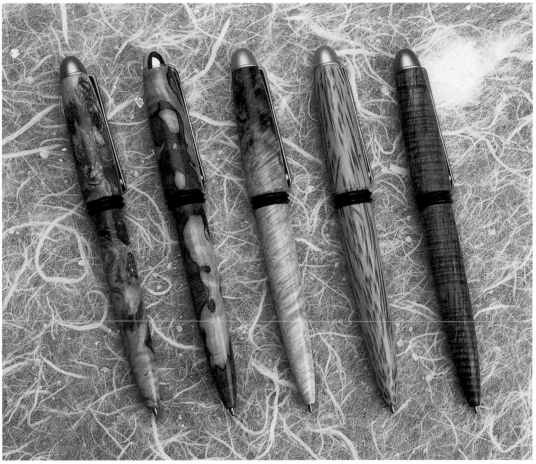

Pens made using the European style kits modified by Rex Burningham to eliminate the metal tips and add blackwood center bands. Materials, from left: spalted buckeye burl, spalted madrone burl, box elder burl, red palm, fiddleback koa.

Pens embellished with pyrography by Brandon Wells. Materials, from left: piqua amerello, bird's-eye maple, pink ivory, bird's-eye maple, pink ivory, bird's-eye maple.

American style pens by Rex Burningham and Kip Christensen. Materials, from left: Environ, spalted buckeye burl, thuya burl, box elder burl, English elm burl, box elder burl, spalted myrtle, amboyna burl.

European style pens by Rex Burningham and Kip Christensen. Materials, from top: spalted holly, putumuju and cocobolo, acetate, Dymondwood, Crushed Velvet, spalted English beech and ebony, Polygem, acetate, box elder burl and ebony.

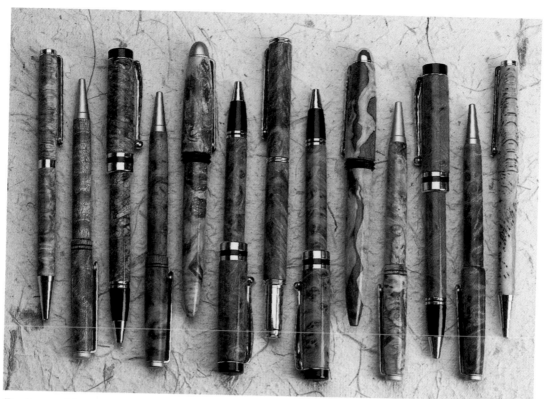

Burls provide some of the most spectacular woods available for turned writing instruments. These pens were turned by Rex Burningham and Kip Christensen from burl woods. All colors are natural. Woods, from left: box elder, myrtle, spalted myrtle, English brown oak, spalted buckeye, amboyna, western maple, thuya, spalted madrone, linden bass, English elm, redwood, honey locust.

Pens showing the natural color contrast between sapwood and heartwood. Rex Burningham and Kip Christensen. Woods, from left: amboyna burl, blackwood, Brazilian rosewood, olive, cocobolo, Burmese rosewood, Carolina cherry, tulipwood, ebony with spalted buckeye burl.

A collage of writing instruments by Rex Burningham and Kip Christensen.

	Twist pen	European/ American style	Tapered Rollerball
Process	Hand-turned T/P	Hand-turned T/P	Hand-turned T/P
Material	Tulipwood T	Stabilized burl, stabilized spalted wood T/P	Dymondwood T
Rip blank	Bandsaw w/rip fence	NA T	Bandsaw w/fence T/P
Crosscut to length	Bandsaw, sliding table T/P	Bandsaw, freehand, w/tape on table T/P	Bandsaw w/gage and slip fence T/P
Storage after cut	Storage tray T/P	Rubber band T/P	Tape T/P
Hold while drilling	Quick grip w/blocks T/P	Gate jig w/base T/P	Parallel jaw clamp T/P
Storage after drilling	Storage tray	Board w/rods T/P	V-groove tray T/P
Glue	Thick CA T/P	Five-minute epoxy T/P	Polyurethane T/P
Glue application	Straw T/P	Make-up brush T/P	Old screwdriver T/P
Hold while trimming	Bench vise T/P	Gate jig T/P	Parallel jaw clamp T/P
Mandrel	Double w/Morse taper T/P	Single w/Morse T, T/P	Points w/drill chuck T/P
Sanding	Standard abrasives T/P	Standard abrasive, not covered	Standard abrasive, not covered
Finish	French polish T/P	Not covered	Plastic polish T/P
Assembly	Bench vise T/P	Drill press (as arbor press) T/P	Drill press w/press jig T/P

T : explained in text

P : shown in photograph

METRIC CONVERSION TABLE

Inches to millimetres and centimetres

mm – millimetres   cm – centimetres

inches	mm	cm	inches	cm	inches	cm
⅛	3	0.3	9	22.9	30	76.2
¼	6	0.6	10	25.4	31	78.7
⅜	10	1.0	11	27.9	32	81.3
½	13	1.3	12	30.5	33	83.8
⅝	16	1.6	13	33.0	34	86.4
¾	19	1.9	14	35.6	35	88.9
⅞	22	2.2	15	38.1	36	91.4
1	25	2.5	16	40.6	37	94.0
1¼	32	3.2	17	43.2	38	96.5
1½	38	3.8	18	45.7	39	99.1
1¾	44	4.4	19	48.3	40	101.6
2	51	5.1	20	50.8	41	104.1
2½	64	6.4	21	53.3	42	106.7
3	76	7.6	22	55.9	43	109.2
3½	89	8.9	23	58.4	44	111.8
4	102	10.2	24	61.0	45	114.3
4½	114	11.4	25	63.5	46	116.8
5	127	12.7	26	66.0	47	119.4
6	152	15.2	27	68.6	48	121.9
7	178	17.8	28	71.1	49	124.5
8	203	20.3	29	73.7	50	127.0

POLYMER CLAY
REFERENCE BOOKS

The New Clay
Nan Roche

Flower Valley Press
Rockville
Maryland
USA

ISBN 0 9620543 4 8

The Art of Polymer Clay
Donna Kato

Watson Guptill Publications
New York
New York
USA

ISBN 0 8230 0278 0

Creating with Polymer Clay
Steven Ford and Leslie Dierks

Lark Books
Asheville
North Carolina
USA

ISBN 0 937274 95 X

ABOUT THE AUTHORS

KIP CHRISTENSEN

Kip Christensen's interest in woodworking began as a result of his father building a cabinet factory in Spokane, Washington, when Kip was 12 years old. He worked at the factory after school and through the summers during his junior high and high school years. While doing undergraduate studies at Brigham Young University, he was introduced to woodturning by Dale Nish. Since then Kip has continued his intense interest in woodturning and has become an accomplished and well-known turner. His work has been published in over a dozen books and displayed in several galleries and exhibitions. He has been an invited presenter for numerous workshops and symposia, and has authored several research and applied articles regarding woodworking and technology education.

Kip is a Professor of Technology Education and coordinator of the woodworking technology program at Brigham Young University. His teaching experience also includes two years at Humboldt State University in Arcata, California. He received a Doctor of Philosophy from Colorado State University in 1991.

While Kip is best known for his lidded containers, he is also comfortable working with bowls, vessels, spindles, and turning production items such as tops and pens. He has pioneered the use of elk and moose antler as a medium for artistic turning. His turnings have been acquired by many private collectors.

Kip and his wife Kim live in Springville, Utah, and are the parents of five children.

REX BURNINGHAM

Rex Burningham was born in Springfield, Massachusetts and reared in Bountiful, Utah. He worked as a carpenter for four years after completing high school. He later attended Brigham Young University on an athletic scholarship for football. While at BYU, working on a degree in technology education, Rex was introduced to woodturning by Dale Nish. During this time he also worked at Craft Supplies USA, a woodturning supply catalog, as an assistant in the woodturning courses. Working alongside some of the world's best-known woodturners, including Dale Nish, Rude Osolnik, Richard Raffan and Ray Key, gave Rex the chance to learn from the best.

After completing his degree, Rex taught woodworking and drafting for three years at East High School in Salt Lake City, Utah.

His work has been published in several magazines and displayed in several galleries and exhibitions. He is a nationally recognized woodturner, teaching and demonstrating throughout the United States.

Currently, Rex is a Vice President of Marketing at Craft Supplies USA. While working for Craft Supplies USA he has the opportunity to research and develop many of the pen kits and woodturning accessories offered today. The combination of his woodturning skills, pen kit development and producing several thousand finished wooden pens makes him one of the most knowledgeable in the field. Rex is also producing and selling woodturnings in fine arts and craft shows across the country.

Rex and his wife Laurie live in Highland, Utah, and are the parents of three children.

INDEX

GMC PUBLICATIONS

BOOKS

WOODCARVING

The Art of the Woodcarver	*GMC Publications*
Carving Birds & Beasts	*GMC Publications*
Carving on Turning	*Chris Pye*
Carving Realistic Birds	*David Tippey*
Decorative Woodcarving	*Jeremy Williams*
Essential Tips for Woodcarvers	*GMC Publications*
Essential Woodcarving Techniques	*Dick Onians*
Further Useful Tips for Woodcarvers	*GMC Publications*
Lettercarving in Wood: A Practical Course	*Chris Pye*
Power Tools for Woodcarving	*David Tippey*
Practical Tips for Turners & Carvers	*GMC Publications*
Relief Carving in Wood: A Practical Introduction	*Chris Pye*
Understanding Woodcarving	*GMC Publications*
Understanding Woodcarving in the Round	*GMC Publications*
Useful Techniques for Woodcarvers	*GMC Publications*
Wildfowl Carving – Volume 1	*Jim Pearce*
Wildfowl Carving – Volume 2	*Jim Pearce*
The Woodcarvers	*GMC Publications*
Woodcarving: A Complete Course	*Ron Butterfield*
Woodcarving: A Foundation Course	*Zoë Gertner*
Woodcarving for Beginners	*GMC Publications*
Woodcarving Tools & Equipment Test Reports	*GMC Publications*
Woodcarving Tools, Materials & Equipment	*Chris Pye*

WOODTURNING

Adventures in Woodturning	*David Springett*
Bert Marsh: Woodturner	*Bert Marsh*
Bill Jones' Notes from the Turning Shop	*Bill Jones*
Bill Jones' Further Notes from the Turning Shop	*Bill Jones*
Bowl Turning Techniques Masterclass	*Tony Boase*
Colouring Techniques for Woodturners	*Jan Sanders*
The Craftsman Woodturner	*Peter Child*
Decorative Techniques for Woodturners	*Hilary Bowen*
Faceplate Turning	*GMC Publications*
Fun at the Lathe	*R.C. Bell*
Further Useful Tips for Woodturners	*GMC Publications*
Illustrated Woodturning Techniques	*John Hunnex*
Intermediate Woodturning Projects	*GMC Publications*
Keith Rowley's Woodturning Projects	*Keith Rowley*
Multi-Centre Woodturning	*Ray Hopper*
Practical Tips for Turners & Carvers	*GMC Publications*
Spindle Turning	*GMC Publications*
Turning Green Wood	*Michael O'Donnell*
Turning Miniatures in Wood	*John Sainsbury*
Turning Pens and Pencils	*Kip Christensen & Rex Burningham*
Turning Wooden Toys	*Terry Lawrence*
Understanding Woodturning	*Ann & Bob Phillips*
Useful Techniques for Woodturners	*GMC Publications*
Useful Woodturning Projects	*GMC Publications*
Woodturning: Bowls, Platters, Hollow Forms, Vases, Vessels, Bottles, Flasks, Tankards, Plates	*GMC Publications*
Woodturning: A Foundation Course (New Edition)	*Keith Rowley*

Woodturning: A Fresh Approach	*Robert Chapman*
Woodturning: A Source Book of Shapes	*John Hunnex*
Woodturning Jewellery	*Hilary Bowen*
Woodturning Masterclass	*Tony Boase*
Woodturning Techniques	*GMC Publications*
Woodturning Tools & Equipment Test Reports	*GMC Publications*
Woodturning Wizardry	*David Springett*

WOODWORKING

Bird Boxes and Feeders for the Garden	*Dave Mackenzie*
Complete Woodfinishing	*Ian Hosker*
David Charlesworth's Furniture-Making Techniques	*David Charlesworth*
Furniture & Cabinetmaking Projects	*GMC Publications*
Furniture Projects	*Rod Wales*
Furniture Restoration (Practical Crafts)	*Kevin Jan Bonner*
Furniture Restoration and Repair for Beginners	*Kevin Jan Bonner*
Furniture Restoration Workshop	*Kevin Jan Bonner*
Green Woodwork	*Mike Abbott*
Making & Modifying Woodworking Tools	*Jim Kingshott*
Making Chairs and Tables	*GMC Publications*
Making Fine Furniture	*Tom Darby*
Making Little Boxes from Wood	*John Bennett*
Making Shaker Furniture	*Barry Jackson*
Making Woodwork Aids and Devices	*Robert Wearing*
Minidrill: Fifteen Projects	*John Everett*
Pine Furniture Projects for the Home	*Dave Mackenzie*
Router Magic: Jigs, Fixtures and Tricks to Unleash your Router's Full Potential	*Bill Hylton*
Routing for Beginners	*Anthony Bailey*
The Scrollsaw: Twenty Projects	*John Everett*
Sharpening Pocket Reference Book	*Jim Kingshott*
Sharpening: The Complete Guide	*Jim Kingshott*
Space-Saving Furniture Projects	*Dave Mackenzie*
Stickmaking: A Complete Course	*Andrew Jones & Clive George*
Stickmaking Handbook	*Andrew Jones & Clive George*
Test Reports: *The Router* and *Furniture & Cabinetmaking*	*GMC Publications*
Veneering: A Complete Course	*Ian Hosker*
Woodfinishing Handbook (Practical Crafts)	*Ian Hosker*
Woodworking with the Router: Professional Router Techniques any Woodworker can Use	*Bill Hylton & Fred Matlack*
The Workshop	*Jim Kingshott*

TOYMAKING

Designing & Making Wooden Toys	*Terry Kelly*
Fun to Make Wooden Toys & Games	*Jeff & Jennie Loader*
Making Wooden Toys & Games	*Jeff & Jennie Loader*
Restoring Rocking Horses	*Clive Green & Anthony Dew*
Scrollsaw Toy Projects	*Ivor Carlyle*
Scrollsaw Toys for All Ages	*Ivor Carlyle*
Wooden Toy Projects	*GMC Publications*

CRAFTS

GARDENING

VIDEOS

MAGAZINES

WOODTURNING ▪ WOODCARVING ▪ FURNITURE & CABINETMAKING
THE DOLLS' HOUSE MAGAZINE ▪ CREATIVE CRAFTS FOR THE HOME
THE ROUTER ▪ THE SCROLLSAW ▪ BUSINESSMATTERS
WATER GARDENING

The above represents a full list of all titles currently published or scheduled to be published.
All are available direct from the Publishers or through bookshops, newsagents and specialist retailers.
To place an order, or to obtain a complete catalogue, contact:

GMC PUBLICATIONS

CASTLE PLACE, 166 HIGH STREET, LEWES, EAST SUSSEX BN7 1XU, UNITED KINGDOM
TEL: 01273 488005   FAX: 01273 478606

Orders by credit card are accepted